P9-DBX-649

Warm Logic

The Art of the Intuitive Lifestyle

SR

Skidmore-Roth Publishing

207 Cincinnati Avenue
El Paso, Texas 79902
915-544-3150

Warm Logic

The Art of the Intuitive Lifestyle

Louis Wynne, Ph.D.
Carolyn S. Klintworth, M.A.

Skidmore-Roth Publishing
El Paso, Texas

Copyright 1990 by Skidmore-Roth Publishing

All rights reserved. No part of this book may be copied or transmitted in any form or by any means without written permission of the publisher.

ISBN 0-944132-11-1

Published by Skidmore-Roth Publishing
207 Cincinnati Avenue
El Paso, Texas 79902

Printed in the United States of America

To *Paul Merced Salcedo*
who lived it

and to Rachel Wynne
"Mere words cannot convey…"

in loving memory

Acknowledgements

Several people have helped us sharpen, clarify, and extend the views embodied in this book, whether together in lengthy discussions with us, in conversations over coffee, on the phone – often at strange hours, or by themselves with the manuscript, pen in hand, making marginal comments. We thank all of them, and absolve them for whatever weaknesses remain: Pat Brey, Michael Dougher, Brooke Dowlen, Spence Dowlen, Kary Goldenberg, Marla Juan-Darien, Bob Klintworth, Maria McEwen, Rosalie Perea, Virginia Ross, Shirley Rubin, Joshua Schneck, Willie Smolak, Judy Schuster, Tim Schuster, Leslie Selwyn, Arthur Sussman, Judith Sussman, Joyce Therkildsen, Mark Wynne, Robyn Wynne, and Sema Wynne.

Most of all, we are indebted to Willard F. Day, Jr., Professor Emeritus of Psychology at the University of Nevada at Reno, who provided much of the inspiration for this book, who commented on it extensively, and whose sudden death prevented the completion of the Foreword which he was writing for it.

Lastly, we express sincere appreciation to Sue Ivey who did the word processing with consummate professionalism and without complaint as we indulged ourselves in making the most minute changes almost up to the moment the manuscript went to press.

Contents

"Man is a microcosm, or a little world, because he is an extract from all the stars and planets of the whole firmament, from the earth and the elements; and so he is their quintessence."

PHILIPPUS AUREOLUS PARACELSUS
(c. 1493-1541)

Introduction

This is a book about feelings. It is about compassion, sensitivity, caring, intimacy, joy, achievement, and fulfillment. It also makes some reference to confusion, anguish, and despair. No book about feelings can restrict itself only to the positive and upbeat, though that is definitely where our emphasis lies.

This is a book about the place of feelings in your life, how they can liberate you from hesitation in your dealings with the world of nature, including the people in it. Rather than portraying feelings as hampering you, as encumbrances and nuisances getting in the way of a rational and logical approach to your problems and difficulties, *Warm Logic* will re-direct your feelings and sensitivities into a harmony with nature.

Warm Logic is the wisdom of nature manifesting itself as wordless guidance. What you will learn in this book is how to hear and feel that guidance when you are both awake and asleep. Actually, you have been hearing and feeling it for a long time but have often been dissuaded from moving with it by all the rules and conventions of our post-industrial, post-Holocaust society. This is the culture which the writer Martin Amis recently called a "moronic inferno," a society which has taught you that every want is a "need," that stress is the inevitable companion of wage-earning, child-rearing, and fulfillment-seeking.

In *Warm Logic* we say, "Not so!" Stress is not "out there" defying us to cope with it. Stress, we will argue, is within you, created out of the ongoing tension between what your own intuitive hunches would have you do, and what the rules laid down by someone in your past are telling you that you are supposed to do, ought not to feel, or what should happen.

1

Unfortunately, most people willingly participate in the creation of stress within themselves. They are easy prey for stress (and anger, guilt, worry, fear) because they have allowed themselves to be convinced by our technological society that it is truly possible to be in control of other people, of themselves, and not only of the present and past, but also of the future. This attitude stems from our Western tradition that humankind is the most perfect part of creation and, therefore, authorized to command and rearrange the rest of nature to our own ends.

Again we say, "Not so!" We will actually argue the opposite: that the first step to liberate your intuitive self, and successfully purge yourself of stress, anger, fear, and the rest, is releasing control, letting go, being vulnerable, and submitting to Nature's way of doing things — in all her realms, human, animal, and inanimate. Since there is, after all, no such thing as "complete control," those who strive for it will always be victim of anger and frustration as things don't work out as expected, as they "should have." Giving up control, we say, ultimately results in attaining the inner peace of invulnerability, confidence, and fulfillment.

Warm Logic was written at a time in the authors' lives that if either of us had been rated on any psychological stress scale, we would have "maxxed it out": deaths within the immediate family, divorce, job changes, and financial crises. Yet, as the book grew, our own symptoms — headaches, back pain, high blood pressure, and skin eruptions — diminished and disappeared. It was as though the book itself had become healer.

This book is not a manual for social change. It is, rather, a guide for your personal ethical and spiritual fulfillment. Warm logic is neither abstract nor theoretical, but very much down-to-earth, its views having been tested, as you will see from our quotations and examples, by many people throughout history. It is a refreshing alternative to a world that is often neither tragic nor comic, just simply grotesque — the only alternative to the bumper sticker philosophy: "Life's a bitch; then you die."

But enough! Your intuitive yearnings have been held in check long enough! Release, let go, and join us in a rediscovered way of living!

Part 1

Warm logic is an approach to living in the Western world during the last quarter of the twentieth century. It is grounded in a sensitivity to and an empathy with Nature and her fundamental workings so intense that no need is felt to rationally explain or to understand those workings. With warm logic, one immediately accepts Nature's immense complexity, mystery and impartiality and that one's actions, thinking, feelings and dreaming are a fundamental part of Nature.

CHAPTER ONE

Chaos and Confusion

*"Tomorrow, and tomorrow, and tomorrow creeps in this petty pace
from day to day to the last syllable of recorded time,
and all our yesterdays have lighted fools the way to dusty death.
Out, out brief candle! Life's but a walking shadow, a poor player
that struts and frets his hour upon the stage and then is heard no more.
It is a tale told by an idiot, full of sound and fury, signifying nothing."*

Macbeth, Act V, Scene V

"God is a comedian playing to an audience that's afraid to laugh."

George Burns
(or was it really Voltaire?)

The world in which you grew up no longer exists. If you are over the age of forty, that world evaporated in the heat and tumult of the decade or so following the assassination of President John F. Kennedy, during which a social revolution was set in motion whose pace continues unabated. If you are not yet forty, you grew, or are growing, to maturity during a time when all of the nation's cherished ideals are being called into question, frequently ridiculed, and often ignored – not so much because they are found wanting, but because all ideals and values are being seen by many as constricting to the spirit of our times.

Some have suggested that ours is a civilization in decline, and certainly many things do not seem to be going too well. Despite all the expansive and expensive programs of President Lyndon John-son's Great Society, our nation is in at least some respects far worse now than, say, in 1950, when the difference between white and black teen-age unemployment was negligible, and overall white un-employment was actually higher than black unemployment. Many aspects of the American scene are grossly changed from those nostalgic days of the 1950's, when the general feeling was that the world could only get better under American leadership, and that an end to world hunger, poverty, illiteracy, and disease was only a few short years away – certainly to be expected before the year 2000. None of this, however, has come to pass. Instead, what has happened has assaulted us with effects devastating to our peace of mind if not our sanity – to our sense of stability, as well as to our ethics, values, and fundamental sense of worth both as individuals and as a nation.

Item: World Leadership. The position of America as leader of at least the free world has changed drastically. We can not accurately posture as the world's moral leader, acting to uphold the highest principles of human dignity in our dealings either with our own citizens or with other nations. Certainly enough has been written about our actions in Viet Nam (the My Lai incident and the use of Agent Orange) to demonstrate that we, like other nations, are capable of atrocities.

Item: Military Position. America's status in the world has also changed with regard to our military prowess. Not only are we any longer the world's unquestioned Number 1 military power, in terms of either quality or quantity; but we have also been humiliated by a fifth-rate power whose soldiers initially wore footgear made from truck tires. We have suffered the indignity of American civilians held hostage for well over a year by a medieval autocrat, this being compounded by our failure to rescue them. And to make our em-barrassment worse, this failure took place well within memory of a heroic if not glamorous rescue by the Israelis of many more of their own hostages on the two-hundredth anniversary of our own in-dependence, in an exploit that Americans had thought was the sort of thing only we were capable of. Who would have thought in 1945 that the world's most feared troops in 1985 would be Jews?

We have also seen the frightful destruction of a U.S. Marine barracks in Beirut, guarded by troops who were not permitted to have their weapons loaded. American heroism is now reduced to Rambo films, but other movies may be more accurate. Audiences a few years earlier had laughed during a scene in *Dr. Strangelove* where Peter Sellers, playing an RAF officer, had to search for a coin to use in a public telephone so that he could communicate vital military information to his headquarters. When the American public was told that one of the commanders on Grenada had to use a personal credit card for the same purpose, no one laughed. When life imitates art, it is rarely funny.

Item: Illiteracy and Ignorance. The United States is now estimated to have an adult illiteracy rate of about 20%, with estimates for the year 2000 as high as 1 in 3 adults (by comparison, Japan's illiteracy rate is 1%). A recent study of America's schoolchildren showed that 40% of 12th graders could not locate Egypt on a map, and 20% could not locate France or China. The National Assessment of Educational Progress in 1986 said that less than 25% of 11th graders could write well enough to succeed in either academia, business, or the professions. The performance of many of their teachers is acknowledged to be little better.

Item: The Litigious Society. There are more lawyers practicing in Chicago than there are in the entire United Kingdom. San Francisco has one attorney for every 60 people, and that proportion is rising rapidly. There is a commensurate rise in the number of laws and regulations to govern our lives, though a fair number of these rules, statutes, and ordinances fall short of their planned effect. Indeed, they frequently make matters worse; the world is far more complicated, obscure, and interdependent than lawyers, legislators, and bureaucrats appear able to comprehend. Consider, for example, how social legislation and regulation over the past three decades have done as much to destroy families as to help them; how related programs have destroyed the social and cultural fabric of inner-city neighborhoods in return for instant high-rise ghettos; and how Drug Enforcement Administration-sponsored spraying of Paraquat on marijuana crops may have been a major cause of the huge growth of cocaine use in the United States in the mid-eighties.

There are even cities in the United States where the criminal justice system appears to have broken down completely.

The civil side of the docket is similarly out of control. Lawyers willing to bring cases for damages in stupendous amounts for a simple fall (Editorial page, *Wall Street Journal*, June 18, 1987) are making us feel rather like the folk of medieval Europe who had to be careful where they put their feet. A stone accidentally kicked could turn out to be a gate to the Underworld, causing the unfortunate soul to be snatched away by demons lurking just below.

In response to more modern demons, many physicians now openly admit to their patients that they are practicing without liability insurance, or that they indulge in the dubious and expensive practice of "defensive medicine," or even leave their profession entirely.

Item: The Professionals and the Experts. Thanks to improvements in sanitation and nutrition over the past hundred years, and a vastly decreased birth-rate, only six out every 100 deaths in the United States are now caused by infectious disease. The leading causes of death (heart disease, cancer, alcoholism, accidents, and suicide) are all derived from a lifestyle characterized by a highly processed "enriched" diet, often eaten "on the run," high in saturated fats, protein, and simple carbohydrates; little exercise; cigarette smoking; noise; overcrowding; air and water pollution; meaningless and unrewarding work in dehumanizing organizations; social and family disorder; random violence; and new virulent forms of sexually transmitted disease.

One out of five adult American women is obese. Of the remaining four, two are significantly overweight, a health-if not life-threatening condition.

It is not surprising, in view of the conditions in which we live, that so many look to alcohol and drugs, legal and illegal, in an attempt to cope. Although estimates vary widely of the number of Americans suffering from serious mental symptoms at some time in their lives, there is no question that a large number of us are "depressed" most of the time. No doubt this is why there are more psychologists, psychiatrists, counselors and therapists in the U.S. than there are firemen – and almost as many as there are policemen.

In discovering that professionals of every stripe are all too frequently not the experts they would have us believe, we are beginning to see the dark humor in the remark of British playwright, George Bernard Shaw, that all professions are conspiracies against the laity. Experts have over the past twenty years told us, for example, how we should raise our children – that the "New Math" and "Reading Readiness" exercises would teach those same children to perform arithmetic and language skills better than ever before; how after-school employment in fast-food restaurants is good for teenagers' sense of responsibility; and that drug use is only a manifestation of adolescent development, and not worthy of our concern.

Even those professionals who do seem to have the public interest at heart often seem inadequate to the task of advising us. It helps our confidence in them little when J. I. Rodale, a nationally-recognized health expert, while touting the advantages of his particular diet, actually dies on camera; when Jim Fixx, the nation's jogging-craze guru has a fatal heart attack in mid-stride; when we learn that the life expectancy of physicians is fifteen years less than the rest of the population; or when we read in the *Wall Street Journal* (July 27, 1988) estimates that well over 200,000 Americans are injured or killed each year as a result of negligence by doctors. And, although we still turn to physicians for advice, we know that theirs is a profession which has become infamous for its insensitivity and distance.

We are not upset by the marvelous technological advances of the past quarter-century; that, for example, we can now buy for less than $5.00 a credit card-sized device which will extract the exact square root of any number in the space of a second or two, while twenty years ago only many repetitive operations on a mechanical device the size of a modern office typewriter could just come close to a number's square root. It is not our technology that overwhelms us, and most of us appear willing to pay the price in waste and inefficiency – since these highly complex devices can only be serviced, if at all, by highly trained specialists. The day is gone when the family car could at least be kept running by an automobile hobbyist, or when we could either start or stop a magazine subscription without having to "allow 6 to 8 weeks."

We are also apparently willing to pay the price for technology in terms of pollution and the degradation of our environment – at least until that pollution touches us personally, such as Love Canal or the New Jersey coast.

It is probably safe to say that, for those sports that interest us, participation is more exhilarating than watching. Even those who can no longer play their favorite sport (or who never could!) will make a habit of "participating" actively from the stands! Yet, according to the *Wall Street Journal*, 25.8 million Americans frequently watch golf on TV. And 26.3 million watch tennis on TV – certainly more than ever played it. This latter sport, one sportscaster labelled as being "as interesting as watching paint dry." Please note that we have nothing against either of these sports – when they are played. What we are suggesting is that there is something very wrong in a society in which so many adults spend so much time neither in active participation nor in actual attendance, but in living-room spectating – a society which, in 1988, would spend over $300 million on X-rated dial-in services.

It is rather the drastic social and demographic changes aggravated by political, economic, and military upheavals on a global scale which send our minds reeling in the search for some sense, some balance, some meaning in it all. What is one to do, to think, to feel?

This book is written to guide you in your search for answers to these and similar questions. It offers you an alternative to the kind of life you have been living, to the kinds of thoughts you have been thinking – even to the distressing feelings you have been plagued with ever since you decided that the world you inherited was beyond all your efforts either to change it, or to live happily and meaningfully in it. We will not encourage you to involve yourself in more and more activities to drown out your feelings of loneliness, meaninglessness, and boredom. We do not see life as a series of problems to be "solved," and we will offer you no "quick fix."

In this book we will teach you how to live an intuitive life style, a life of direct – not vicarious – experiences, a truly lovely world free of the arbitrary rules and imposed values which were only the beginning of your frustrations. Such a life style – available to anyone who wants it – will be open to your best efforts at achievement and happiness, to spontaneity of self-expression, to new feelings of personal worth, now.

At the end of this book, you will emerge from a learning experience which has shown you a different view of your place in the world, a view that will at once constitute the beginning of a new life of confidence and competence, of personal accomplishment and contentment. It will be a life in which your serenity will be an example for others to emulate as you and they begin to create the microcosm of a better world, free of fickle social pressures to conform, free of the fads and fashions clouding our vision, the noise and narcissism, the waste and pollution, the posturing and pretense...the sound and the fury felt by us all.

Summary

The world, or at least the part of it that we live in and love called the United States of America, seems to be in a hell of a mess. It appears to be no place to raise children, and certainly no place to have any sense of stability, or security, or meaning, or confidence. We are inundated by drugs, violence, and epidemic venereal disease – as well as by professionals, bureaucrats, and media types who claim at least to "have a handle" on the situation.

How can you deal with all this? Will things eventually "settle down"? Can you live a life free of stress, a life of meaning – amid this clamor, chaos, and confusion?

Yes, you can, though it will be you, aided by warm logic, who will do the "settling down" – to a meaningful, potentially stress-free life. This new life will affect others and cause a ripple effect, bringing stability to all that surround you.

CHAPTER TWO

Warm Logic: The Birth of Intuitive Action

"Fay que vouldras!"
("Do what you want!")

Rabelais

"Nothing worth knowing can be understood with the mind."

Woody Allen

"Seek not to understand what is too difficult for you,
search not for what is hidden from you.
Be not over-occupied with what is beyond you,
for you have been shown more than you can understand."

Apochrypha (Ben-Sira)

Living intuitively involves achieving an intimate sensitivity to the world, submitting yourself to the entire spectrum of things both as they operated in the past and as they are operating now. It involves your paying attention not just to the one thing or the one set of circumstances existing right now, but to all sets of circumstances that have ever happened to you.

When people pay attention to something, when they concentrate, they often notice a feeling of increased tension as if they were straining to take in as much information as possible. Tension, however, is an obstacle to a truly sensitive state. If, for example, you want to pay close attention to someone else, to what that person

13

is thinking and feeling, as well as to what he or she is doing, such as when you want to sympathize with one person's grief, understand another's confusion, negotiate agreement with a third's stubbornness, or empathize with a fourth person's fears, what you must actually do is relax in your attempt to crawl inside the other's skin, to meet the person where he or she is.

Being intuitive, said most simply, means playing it by ear, winging it, going with your guts, crossing your bridges when you get to them, going with the flow, and leaving well enough alone. It is knowing, as you complete a purchase, that what you've bought is exactly what you were looking for — in color, style, and design. It is knowing that you've made a key entry error without needing to look either at the keyboard or the typewritten page for verification. And, when it comes to following directions, the intuitive person is more likely to puzzle her way through the procedure and then write the directions herself, afterwards. It is presumably what the English do when they "muddle through." It must be emphasized, though, that this does not mean dealing frivolously, capriciously, or even amorally with life. On the contrary, submitting yourself to the conditions and demands of the world around you will be, at least at first, frightening to you, but such submission is anything but capricious because Nature's demands and conditions themselves, while often incredibly subtle, are anything but capricious. If we think that the world is governed by chance, it is because of our very limited understanding of it. As Albert Einstein said, "God does not throw dice." There is truly an order in Nature, though we can rarely express just what that order is.

Because we will be using the term "contingencies" frequently throughout the remainder of the book, we'll take a moment here to define it. The contingencies in a situation are Nature's demands and conditions. They refer to how the world reacts impartially to whatever we do in a situation. For example, the contingencies imposed on us by a coke machine operate as follows: When we put two quarters in the slot, and we press a particular button, a certain kind of container is delivered to us. Further, if a red light has been turned on before we put our money in, this just-described contingency will not operate. This example is a very simple contingency, but all contingencies operating in our world work the same way. They all have three parts: (1) Some equivalent of the coke machine; (2) some action on our part; and (3) the equivalent in the particular situation of the container of soda pop. Any departure from either (1) or (2) will fail to produce (3). Putting the two quarters into a mail-box will not produce a can of soda pop, neither will putting rubles or pesos into an American soda machine.

Nature's contingencies are, of course, incredibly more obscure, complex, and difficult to figure out. For example, they make simple by comparison choices within the air traffic control situation at Chicago-O'Hare on Thanksgiving; a 4th down and one situation against a very strong defense, on your own 35 yard line, with two minutes to play, and the score 14-12 against you in the Super Bowl; or in any of a number of situations you could envision in poker, chess, backgammon, baseball, or at your place of employment.

The most important contingencies, either natural or contrived by humans (such as the coke machine), are experienced by you as feelings. You can see, hear, smell, taste, and touch the events and things (what those events and things are being highly arbitrary) in your world, but the relations between them, Nature's demands and conditions, are felt. Traditionalists have referred to this as the process of logical inference, to distinguish it from the simple description of events, but we are saying something quite *different*. We are saying that the situation in which you are most *sympatico* with Nature is one not logical and rational at all — neither descriptive nor inferential. Logic and reason are verbal and linguistic reconstructions of Nature and they all too frequently obstruct your intimacy with Her.

Contingencies are not always effective immediately. They can take years to have an effect, depending either on their subtlety or on our sensitivity to them, based on our past experience with them. It often takes a while for things to "dawn on us," for us to "catch on to" what is happening. If the coke machine were changed one morning to require an additional nickel, it wouldn't take you long to accommodate it — even if the service person forgot to change the sign on the front of the machine. Whether or not our earth is indeed in a long-term warming trend; whether or not you really are pregnant; whether your new business venture is indeed off to a healthy start; or whether a new and promising relationship really is what it seems to be are all possible now-occurring changes in Nature to which it will take you longer to catch on.

There is no single guaranteed technique or set of techniques which you can use to achieve a high degree of sensitivity to your world. Some people have suggested that it is necessary to sit in a certain position. Others say that only through fasting, or the use of certain drugs, or infliction of discomfort or pain on oneself, can one attain true sensitivity. Whatever techniques you think you must use to listen to, to hear and, most of all, to feel the world in all its subtleties and nuances, the emphasis is the same: to become so sensitive to those contingencies that you then act in the most effective and confident way in dealing with them.

It is vital to keep in mind that achieving this awareness does not consist in the doing of anything. To do anything, in the sense of following a recipe is to do something, and what you most want to do here is nothing. You want to do by not-doing, to achieve a level of sensitivity by not-doing; by not-thinking most of all, but also by not-talking (but saying what needs to be said), not listening (but hearing everything), and not-sniffing (but smelling everything). You are then free to feel what the universe's contingencies would have you feel. These same contingencies will at the same time prompt action in you. You will then get up, and do.

Not-doing is referred to by some people as meditation. We feel that it is much more — that is, if one thinks of meditation as fundamentally sitting motionless. Not-doing is permitting yourself to become maximally sensitive to present contingencies while minimizing the effects of your thinking about what you ought to do in the situation. And this can be done whether you are sitting or walking, driving a car or standing in line, playing a guitar or pounding a nail.

To repeat, achieving a state of sensitivity involves the removing of obstacles and not the assertive pursuit of a meditative state. Hugh Prather, in *There Is a Place Where You Are Not Alone*, says that he has never liked the techniques usually considered essential in meditation. He suggests, on the contrary, just sitting in a chair and listening for a few minutes. This will result, he says, in your eventually feeling that you are being given dictation, though without sound — an account remarkably similar to that of Moses writing the Ten Commandments (God wrote them through Moses); or the way the ancient Greeks viewed creativity in the arts (one or another of the muses wrote the poetry or the song through the artist. It was the artist's task to let the muse be heard.)

What happens when "the muse is heard?" What does it look like? One example is how you feel when watching an expert performing his or her craft so well that it is made to look easy. When you watch, say, Maestro Vladimir Horowitz at the piano, it is easy to get the impression that his hands are playing by themselves! This effect on you is enhanced when Mr. Horowitz turns toward the audience and laughs with the joy of the music while his hands do not miss a single note! Whether you are watching an expert carpenter, seamstress, racing driver, mechanic, painter, sculptor, skier, basketball player, singer, or poet, the effect on us is the same. Our impression is that the performance is effortless, that the person is not trying at all; that the cabinet, gown, or painting is creating itself; that the poem or book is writing itself; and not under the performer's control at all but under the control of something else.

And it is! Whether it is the performance of the skier, of the pianist, of the painter who tells us that "the painting will tell me when it is finished," of the entranced or possessed participant in a religious service, or even of ourselves in normal conversation, the control is the same. It is the control exerted by Nature's contingencies, sometimes specially arranged in advance by ourselves or by others, but always present.

If you balk at the idea that your voice is somehow different in the way it operates from your hands; that is, that your voice is controlled by your mind while the skill of your hands is controlled by feedback from the environment, ask yourself this question. Have you ever said something ("blurted it out") and then immediately followed what you had said with, "I didn't mean to say that. It just came out. Something just took hold of me."? Of course you have! Well, what was it that "just took hold of you"? It was the very powerful contingencies operating in the situation; and, when someone says something that you were "just about to say," it is not a case of that person's "reading your mind." It is that both of you are being influenced at that moment by the identical set of contingencies.

The Western version of things teaches us otherwise. It has taught us that first we think, then we act — at least most of the time. But where do thoughts come from? They come not from somewhere in the brain; there is no known process whereby neurons firing in the cerebral cortex themselves create thought. Although the search for such a process has gone on for many decades, it has been fruitless. As long ago as 1937, the great neuropsychologist Karl Lashley, in finally giving up his own search for some change in the patterns of nerve structure resulting from recently learned tasks, said, obviously tongue-in-cheek, "I sometimes feel that learning just is not possible." In effect, what he was saying was that although his experimental subjects were clearly changing their behaviors as a result of his procedures, he could find no neural counterparts to those changes. No one has since.

Where, then, do thoughts come from? They come from the contingencies in the situations in which we live. They are in a very real sense those contingencies talking to us. When the mystic, Eknath Easwaran, said, "We do not think our thoughts; they think us," he was absolutely correct! Indeed, he might have said the same thing about dreams and about the racing thoughts and hallucinations of the schizophrenic, for they, too, are contingencies talking to us — and the more subtle, vague, or chaotic they are, the more weird the dreams and hallucinations!

When we look physically inside people's heads for "thoughts," we will never find them because we are looking in the wrong place! And no highly developed technology such as Computed Axial Tomography (CAT) scans will do for us in that search what lesser techniques have failed to do. Thoughts are a product of these subtle, complex, ineffable, even mystical contingencies of the world in which we are immersed.

You will not always think before you act; you will, perhaps more often — just act. One individual said it this way: "Things happen, then you sit around trying to figure out why you did what you did." One of our purposes in writing this book is to make you as comfortable with such "thoughtless" action, both in yourself and in others, as was the great Yogi Berra when he said, "How can you think and hit at the same time?" And we want to teach you techniques for making sure that such actions are not capricious, precipitous, or unduly hazardous.

Our examples: Moses writing the Ten Commandments, the Greek muses, Maestro Horowitz' playing, and your own verbal faux pas, are all products of the strong control which current environmental contingencies have over your actions without your realizing it. Further, these products are examples of the workings of the Taoist principle of wu-wei, of doing by *not-doing*, of "actionless action," of submitting oneself completely to the action of current and past contingencies without attempting to control them; indeed, of explicitly yielding up all control to them.

It is this shedding of any desire to control which renders it impossible for the expert in any field to say how he or she does those miraculous things with hands or voice. The acts themselves do indeed appear to be miracles; they are beyond all attempts at analysis! This is why it is futile to ask the truly expert, in any field of endeavor, how his or her skill came about. And it is why the expert's answer always sounds incomplete, if not silly. Remember Muhammad Ali's remarks at his before-the-fight weigh-ins about why he was such an admittedly great heavyweight? Perhaps his most lucid answer was, "...float like a butterfly; sting like a bee!" Casey Stengel, one of the most successful baseball managers of all time (helped considerably, of course, by having quite a stable of hitters), explained his virtuosity with such elegant analyses as, "They say you can't do it, but sometimes it doesn't always work."

Such statements never do justice to an artist's creative genius. Laurence Olivier, one of the greatest actors of our century, thought of himself as only "a diligent, expert workman" and his art as "just" technique. The dying words of Ludwig van Beethoven, composer of such monumental works as *Fidelio* and his *Ninth Symphony*, were the question: "I had a little talent, didn't I?"

It is futile to speculate in any way about how the truly great creative and intuitive writers, artists, performers in the arts and in sports achieve their unique mastery, and any number of Western philosophers have failed in their attempts to reduce creativity to rules of logic or "scientific method." We cannot, given the very nature of intuitive action, tell what fortuitous, subtle – even acci- dental – arrangement of contingencies, rules, or other categories or patterns of events brought Vladimir Horowitz, Isaac Newton, Rodin, Mikhail Baryshnikov, Michelangelo, Mozart, Frank Lloyd Wright, Shakespeare, Rembrandt, Itzhak Perlman, Einstein, and a host of others from their first involvement with their craft to new heights of creation.

How does one do without doing? We can only say how one begins. Once the scene is set, anything is possible. First, assume that everyone else is already not-doing. They are already acting on the basis of how they see the contingencies of their world operat- ing, and you must willingly forgive them for their not-doing.

Modern oriental martial arts suggest two principles which are derived from wu-wei. The first is *mizu no kokoro* – a mind like water, suggesting qualities of calmness and reflection. The second is *tsuki no kokoro* – a mind like the moon, referring to the need to be constantly aware of the totality of the situation, just as moon- light shines equally on everything.

It is no doubt these qualities of calmness, reflection and aware- ness which prompt westerners to describe those people practiced in meditation as inscrutable and imperturbable. They seem so im- mersed in the world surrounding them, a world which includes us ourselves, that that world appears to contain no surprises for them. This is no better brought home to us than in the film *The Seven Samurai*, when one of the warriors enters a house where an attacker is waiting in ambush behind a door. Even as the attacker strikes, his blow is blocked by the raised arm of the samurai – who does not even turn his head to look at his attacker! His warding off the blow appears to take place without either thought or excessive activity.

The universe and its contingencies act on you every moment of your waking and sleeping life. All you need to do is move with them in their totality without embarrassment or apology, without re- quiring of yourself that you can say what they are. The contingencies speak silently to you, telling you what to do and when. All you have to do is ask the question then wait to feel the answer. There are no directions written on the package called The Universe.

We have called this intuitive approach to life, this Taoist approach of wu-wei, warm logic — to differentiate it from the "cold" logic of the Greek-Christian intellectual tradition which emphasizes rationality, data, inference, analysis, and verbal reconstructions of our world. Warm logic incorporates words like sensitivity, intimacy, and subjectivity, and emphasizes comfort with our choices and actions as opposed to the accuracy, precision, replication, objectivity, and distance prized by "cold" logic. Warm logic is arguing by demonstration rather than by description, by simile rather than by metaphor, by citing concrete experiences rather than by statistical inference, trends, and projections computer-extrapolated from masses of data. It is eminently practical rather than theoretical, narrative rather than explanatory, suggestive rather than prescriptive, subjective rather than deductive, qualitative rather than quantitative, intimate rather than vicarious. It welcomes surprise rather than demanding guarantees. It is as much art as science.

The unwillingness to give reasons why one is doing something is what causes trouble for people reared and educated in the Greek-Christian tradition. Note the patronizing tone of these examples. From a book review in the *Wall Street Journal* (August 13, 1987): "In most cases the authors give only intuitive evidence for why transaction costs should be high or low, and their intuitions…are rather blithe." In a recent book on the use by lawyers of the insanity plea as a defense strategy for their clients, the author stated that, "professionals often cling to beliefs about the insanity defense that rest on intuition, misinformation, or ideology."

Westerners have trouble with such statements as that by R. G. H. Siu who says that the essences of reality are inexpressible in words; or as that by the Buddhist master Asvaghosa who said, "All things in their fundamental nature are not nameable or explicable. They cannot be expressed in any form of language." What such statements are attempting to convey is that when you try to describe, to analyze, to try to understand by means of rules or of any rational verbal process, you limit yourself to that analysis; you

21

limit yourself to an understanding grounded in your own words and constructs.

Siu's answer lies in what he calls the allusive-negative approach. With this technique, the phenomenon of interest is not examined directly, but extraneous aspects of it are stripped away as the object is investigated. The object is never described or analyzed. But, when all inconsequential aspects have been removed, the phenomenon remains, without ever being spoken of, in its pristine condition.

Take, for example, the Western way of describing to a realtor the house you want to buy. Westerners say, "We want an 1800-square foot, 3-bedroom, 2-bath house with a 2-car attached garage in the Glenwood Hills Subdivision." By contrast, the allusive-negative approach proceeds by excluding all non-wanted characteristics: homes with 1 and 2-bedrooms, 4 or more bedrooms; houses with other than a two-car garage; and homes not in the Glenwood Hills Subdivision. When all the non-wanted characteristics have been eliminated, just as the tough and bitter outer leaves of an artichoke are discarded to get at the pulpy inner leaves and heart, the house of one's desires emerges without ever having been actually described.

This approach is not at all the assertive, analytic, manipulative, experiment-oriented way students of the Western scientific tradition have been taught to approach problems. Such people have been taught to be, first and foremost, rational and logical when working unfamiliar territory. Indeed, until very recently, most writers have portrayed western culture as seeing sensitivity to contingencies as intruding on rational thinking, and as interfering with the proper way of making decisions.

In this book we are taking the exact opposite position. Particularly in their really important decisions, we would like our readers to rely much less on cold logic, reason and data. We feel that truly crucial life decisions should never be approached rationally, and that to attempt to do so quickly raises the spectre of having to live with the consequences of an action with which one was never comfortable from the beginning.

In deciding whether to have a baby, whether to get divorced after twenty years of marriage (now that the children are grown), whether to continue pouring money into a beloved old car, or whether to hold onto an investment which paid off well in the past (but not recently), one is tempted to make lists of pros and cons, and even to ask the advice of others about what should go on those lists. This seems to give the decision to cut one's losses a rational and quantifiable basis, amenable to logical argument and reasoning.

However, having a baby, staying married (or getting a divorce), quitting your job, or keeping a car is not rational, no matter how hard some authors have tried to make it so (see, for example, Merle Bombardieri's *The Baby Decision*). That is why, having examined your lists of pros and cons, you use warm logic and throw out the long list containing the reasons for acting one way, and you go the other – just because it feels right. And, haven't you noticed that when you do, for example, quit your job and head out in a new direction with only your guts guiding you, you do not feel afraid – even though you don't know how you'll pay next month's rent!

In such "decisions," reasons and data carefully analyzed, don't help. In fact, since rationality, analysis, and data are so closely tied to the idea of decision-making in our culture, perhaps we should dispense with the term entirely. Let's call it choosing, instead.

A particular course of action recommended by "cold" logic will not feel right because your past, as it is now making itself felt, is giving you a different message from that careful and cold analysis. But it is your past, and your present, that you should be listening to the most – not your calculations or some set of rules. As the French novelist and philosopher Jean-Paul Sartre said "Willed deliberation is always faked...when I deliberate the die is already cast."

How can you know, though, when you are acting on the basis of rules, or out of your intuitive leanings? You can tell by the way you feel. Acting from rules leaves you frustrated, uncomfortable, at worst depressed and invalidated, and, at best, complacent. Acting intuitively exhilarates you!

But, you may say, that might be irresponsible! Not so; actions only become "irresponsible," even pathological, when the individual is protected from the consequences of his or her acts. That is, when the person is shielded from the natural flow of the contingencies produced by his or her own actions. This is the case,

for example, when parents protect their children from the consequences of drunk driving—even when no one is hurt, and permit
the only consequence to be a DWI citation by a policeman. A similar example, again in child-rearing, is the child's staying out late
against parental advice, not doing homework for school the next
day, and then asking the parent to call the school to say that he or
she is sick. If the parent gives in to the child, the child is protected
from the natural consequences contingent on his or her behavior:
the censure of the teacher, the embarrassment, perhaps also the
extra "make-up" work. The long-term consequences of this sort of
child-rearing can result in the adolescent labelled "conduct disordered" or the adult labelled "antisocial personality."

In the current jargon of those who treat alcohol and substance
abusers, people who protect others from the consequences of their
addictive behaviors are called enablers. That is, they enable the
substance abuser, unwittingly encouraging dependency and other
dysfunctional actions, to continue his or her addiction. Some
therapists go so far as to say enablers need to be protective so that
they become co-dependent on alcohol without having imbibed
one drop.

When actions flow from intuitive sources, rather than from
decisions and thinking, these actions are actually more responsible, not less. Intuitive actions are "responsible" to their supporting
contingencies; rule-regulated acts are "responsible" to the person or
persons who influenced your thinking and concocted those rules.

The reasons and rules governing your actions are ultimately
derived from contingencies that operated on you, yourself, or that
operated on someone else—such as a parent. Rules are subordinate
to contingencies, and it is the wise person who keeps that in mind.

Remember your frustration as a youth in school when you discovered that our very language has few if any hard and fast rules?
"'I' before 'E' except after 'C'," is one of the more universal rules, yet
it has its exceptions; and it is sometimes all right to put a preposi-
tion at the end of a sentence (Winston Churchill once said of this
rule, "This is the sort of arrant nonsense up with which I will not
put!"). Why aren't there universal rules of language? Why must

children not only learn the rules but also the many exceptions and, most important, how do they do that?

The reason that there are no universal rules of language is that language develops without the guidance of rules; indeed sometimes in actual contravention of those rules that have already been constructed by grammarians to describe its current shape. Sometimes it is even youth themselves who mold and modify it. So the rules are always playing a game of catch-up. This is true whether we are talking about our language or our customs and social conventions. You learn language as you learn everything else – by being exposed to the world and its contingencies. The rules, the analyses, come much later, and often not at all.

There is a story told of Admiral Horatio Nelson, one of England's immortal military heroes who, at the Battle of Copenhagen, was pressing his ship forward to exploit the tactical advantage when he was told by a subordinate that the fleet flagship was sending a signal that he should pull back. Nelson, being much closer to the action than the fleet admiral, was thereby more sensitive to the contingencies of the situation, and he knew that to withdraw at that point would have been unwise. He therefore put his telescope to the eye which he had lost to a musket ball during an earlier engagement, and said, "What signal to withdraw? I see no such signal!" And he fought on to win a decisive victory.

American military men have also learned a similar respect for intimacy with the contingencies of a situation. This is why they have contempt for people – usually junior officers – who "do things by the book," that is, whose actions are regulated by rules rather than by a non-analytic but thorough familiarity with situations.

When this crucial point is forgotten, when rules are imposed on others in contravention to powerful contingencies, trouble starts. For example, when a law is passed making it a punishable offense to drive an automobile faster than 55 miles per hour, one can expect that law to be largely ignored because of the potent contingencies supporting our driving at much faster speeds. These contingencies supporting faster driving are much stronger and more consistent than the state-imposed competing contingencies which punish fast driving.

Another much more troublesome example concerns the trafficking in and consumption of illegal drugs. What law-makers and other rule-givers apparently do not understand is that no law prohibiting either the distribution, possession, sale, or consumption of illegal drugs will ever be obeyed unless the strong contingencies supporting this distribution (tremendous profits) or use (exhilarating "highs") are altered. One demonstration that bureaucrats do on occasion realize the importance of such contingencies was the remark by Doris Meissner, a former acting commissioner of the U.S. Immigration and Naturalization Service, when she said (*Wall Street Journal*, November 6, 1987), "We are not going to eliminate illegal immigration. *The underlying forces are too strong.*" [emphasis added]

These are the underlying forces that warm logic is putting you in touch with. These are Nature's demands and conditions, Her ever-operating contingencies within whose harmony your actions will lie as you adopt the intuitive lifestyle.

Summary

Your actions are intuitive when they are sensitive to the entire situation you are dealing with — including your entire past experience with similar situations. You cannot achieve such sensitivity by following a rigid set of procedures, such as a recipe or a manual, a formula, or even a computer program. On the contrary, the way to proceed is to not-do, to act without feeling the need to understand why you are doing what you are doing — to let the contingencies in the situation, and in all previous similar situations, carry you.

Intuitive actions will maximize your contentment. That is why the most important decisions in your life must not be made rationally: "I know what I should do (cold logic), but I want to do something else (warm logic)."

CHAPTER THREE

Inventorying the Present

"The obscurest epoch is today."

Robert Louis Stevenson

*"We are here and it is now.
Further than that
all human knowledge is moonshine."*

H. L. Mencken

The following exercise is a practical demonstration of warm logic. It is your introduction to how it feels to act intuitively. We want you to describe to yourself, in detail, every aspect of the entire situation in which a current and pressing problem lies. Think of the entire cast of characters involved with your problem, the constraints of the situation, the history of the problem as it developed, earlier attempts at solutions, and the suggested solutions of other people. After you have taken as much time as you need to do this, continue with this chapter. Yes, we are leaving you hanging, but you will understand why at the end of the chapter.

Let us suppose that you have just inherited a modest amount of money, and after indulging a few long-stifled whims that you could not until now afford, you have a little money left which you decide to invest. How do you approach this pleasant problem? Let us look at some possible approaches.

You could, of course, ask the advice of someone, either an expert or a friend. Such a person presumably "knows the market" and can tell you in what investments your money is likely to do well. This is not really an answer to your problem, however, because you then must answer just how your expert or friend arrived at those recommendations.

There are two basic approaches to the problem. In practice, these are not exclusive of one another, but we will deal with them separately as though they were. The techniques are used just as much in selling as they are in buying a particular investment. The first way is to attempt to guess what will happen in certain sectors of the economy over the period of time you want to have the money "tied up." To do this, you look at forecasts, predictions, and prognostications, and you attempt to project trends into the future. In each case you estimate the risk of loss as well as the chances of gain. From these data you then decide those specific investments in which to become involved. This approach is as rational, logical, and data-based as it can be. The second way is to inventory the present for each sector of the economy in which you are interested, to enumerate and examine in as much detail as you can, what is going on now. This detail would include not only the price/earnings ratio of a particular stock as well as the price itself, but all the data on the company that you can get your hands on — certainly beyond what is available to you in the company prospectus: employee absenteeism rate due to sickness, "water-cooler" gossip, the hot agenda items at the last board meeting, or whether or not the company's sales head has spoken about leaving. Some of these items are impossible to obtain from a practical point of view. They are included here only to bring home the point: the more current information you have, the better, including gross market movements such as the October 19, 1987 crash, as part of the context within which your projected investment has moved.

Now, you may ask, isn't some information more important than other? Is it not possible that you'll be inundated by useless mounds of data? Isn't the price/earnings ratio more important than the upcoming marriage of the CEO's daughter? Maybe. There is no sure-fire formula for investment success any more than for scientific discovery or musical creativity. That is to say, whatever it takes to be creative, or successful in an investment program, or intuitive in any way, is not reducible to a formula. Just as the painting tells the painter when it is finished, just as the musical score tells the composer that no further refinements will improve it (thus leading a Beethoven not to write a *4th Leonore Overture* but, instead, to create a new composition, the *Overture to Fidelio*), so the available data tells the sensitive and intuitive investor what to do and when. The important thing, then, is to immerse yourself in the data, surround yourself with it over as long a period of time as can be conveniently arranged; but do not think about the problem! Do not ruminate over it. Do not analyze it. It is your extended experience with how the marketplace works that you are trying to bring to the surface. It is this past which will tell you what to do, whether or not you can make sense of it.

It is important for you to realize that studying the history of a particular index, say, the Silver/Gold ratio, is not the same as having actually lived through these same price fluctuations. The difference is reading someone's autobiography as opposed to living his or her life. The issue is not that the history of some index is itself no reliable indicator of its future movement, though that is certainly true. It is that there is no substitute for your experiencing the world itself. You cannot develop an intuitive awareness, sensitivity, and effectiveness by reading either stock charts or autobiographies.

The enumeration of a situation as in an inventory of the present is a sort of way-station on your route to a more intuitive dealing with your world. It is a device for increasing your involvement with the here-and-now rather than with your hopes, wishes, goals, dreams, and fears for the future, or with your regrets over the past. Eventually, your explicit inventorying of the present will become so automatic that you will not even realize you're doing it. That is when you will truly begin an intuitive life style, and permit yourself to submit to a situation, to be vulnerable to your past experience with similar situations, whether or not there is a specific problem at hand to be dealt with, without apprehension that the actions prompted by the present situation will not be in your best interest, or not what you "really want."

When you do not inventory the present, when you abandon the present for either the past or the future, you perpetuate all that is negative in your life. Preoccupation with the past involves holding on to hurt and loss; it involves recrimination, regret, sorrow, anger, and the counting up of "mistakes." A preoccupation with the future, although it often involves hope, more frequently has an aura of impatience, apprehension, worry, and fear. Without exception, people who refuse to live in the present will convey to the world anxiety and disappointment and, in so doing, they will continue to build a longer past of ineffectiveness on which to dwell with misgivings.

The way to emerge from this rut is to live in, and deal with, what is going on right now — to refuse to ruminate and torture yourself with what might happen in some fictitious future. And, you can start doing that immediately — if not today, then tonight. You can start seeing your dreams as your current inventory of the present.

We believe that dreams are our most intimate experience of Nature's workings, and that interpreting them is, at least in principle, not difficult at all; it certainly does not require us to create some mysterious entity such as an "unconscious mind" to account for them. First, let us agree to put aside obvious examples such as how your dream of being caught in a snowstorm is brought about by sleeping near an open window during winter; your dream that the telephone is ringing while the alarm radio is buzzing; or the incorporation into the ongoing dream of a subject in a sleep laboratory of the image of a bowl of soup when the investigator whispers, "bowl of soup." (The investigator knows that the subject is dreaming because of rapid eye movements.) The open window, the alarm radio, and the investigator's whisper are all easily-specified events participating in very simple contingencies — much like those represented by the Coke machine mentioned earlier — and the resulting dream images easily understood. Natural contingencies, however, particularly as they operate in your social "transpersonal" life, are incredibly more complicated and obscure. That is why your dreams in response to them are usually, in practice, so difficult to interpret.

We suggest that the images you "see" in your dreams, and the sounds and voices that you "hear," are all things you were actually seeing and hearing, either in the flesh or in a film, the last time you were feeling as you are feeling now. The connecting link between that earlier time and now is the similarity of the contingencies operating, that is, the similarity of the feelings prompted by those similar contingencies. It is your present feelings which evoke the images of the events, people, and places accompanying similar feelings at an earlier time.

The images seen in dreams are not of things that are going to happen; they are not portents of the future. They are of things that have already happened. In other words, not only are your feelings a highly sensitive response to whatever circumstances surround you, but also your body seems to have the ability, when similar circumstances evoke those same feelings, to also bring back visual images of what was happening then.

To interpret a dream, you begin by asking how you felt during that dream. Any of the common descriptions will do: happy, sad, apprehensive, grief-stricken, terrified, hurried, lost, incapable, or threatened. Then ask yourself when you felt this way before. Lastly, ask yourself what events and contingencies were happening then. Your answer to this last question is also a statement of the contingencies operating on you now, and what brought about the dream. It is, of course, difficult to answer, in words, the question, "When did I last feel this way?" How we "answer" that question—without actually asking it—is to dream about that last time. What we "see" is the answer: the near-identical situation in the past.

Being asleep has one important effect on your feelings which you have certainly noticed yourself: they are often amplified and experienced far more intensely in dreams than when you are awake. This is because when you are awake, your feelings are dampened by ongoing sensory input through your eyes, ears, and other organs from the many events happening to you moment by moment as you move about, talk, eat, drive your car, and perform your job. Therefore you are not as sensitive to the relationships between those events, what we have been calling the contingencies of your world. When you are asleep, however, just as to some

31

degree when you meditate, those relationships have full sway over your feelings because they are unimpeded by sensory input from the events in your surroundings—since your eyes are closed, your hands relaxed, your mouth empty, and your whole body still.

Do not be surprised if, while waiting to meet the woman your son has told you he is serious about, you dream about your very first day at school (when you were about to meet your teacher). Or if, after having bought a new car following a long search for just the right color, you dream about searching for a jacket of the same color you need to have for a special occasion. (Note that in the dream the wanting of the right-colored car gets translated into the need for the right-colored jacket: the emotional level is heightened in the dream.)

Remember, though, the search for the jacket is not something you are going to do in the future; it is not a premonition. It is something very close to what you once did, and it is now being recalled by the similarity of the circumstance. Dreaming is always *deja vu*. Rather than a mere preoccupation with the past, it is your using of the past to intuit the present.

When you do not recognize the people or places in a dream, it is because the last time you were feeling as you are feeling now you were not seeing the people involved clearly, perhaps because you were very young, or because you were not paying attention to those details of a situation. Another way of saying this is that the actual identities of the people in your dream may be irrelevant to the contingencies producing those images; any human image will do to satisfy the contingency.

It may also be that whatever contingencies are operating in your life (and therefore in your dream) can be satisfied by any living thing; and so a pet cat or dog can appear "instead of" a human if it has prompted in you, in circumstances similar to those currently existing, feelings like those you are now having toward a person. In such a way you may, on the occasion of your daughter's graduation with honors from high school or college, dream about your dog taking best-of-show at a prestigious meet.

Lastly, your inability to recognize one or more of the people in your dream may be because you have mis-identified the current operating contingencies in your life, and the pattern of emotions they are prompting. You are, as a result, searching the wrong time in your past for their counterpart.

This view of dreaming tells you why, when you dream, you are so often a child again. It is because the last time you felt the way you do now – the last time a highly similar set of contingencies was impacting on you – you were indeed a child. This view also tells you why, no matter how much you'd like to have a dream on a particular topic or about a particular person, you usually can't. Dreams are Nature's contingencies talking to you; you cannot command them what to say. In that sense, dreams are like the "mirror on the wall" in the story of Snow White which told who was the "fairest of them all": your dreams tell you the straight truth, not necessarily what you want to hear. The good side of this is the security you feel knowing that what you've been told is undistorted by wishful thinking or biased data analysis!

People who habitually use intuitive approaches to life's challenges frequently have to apologize for their inability to logically explain how these approaches work. What these intuitive people do when they are being intuitive seems always to be looked upon with suspicion and doubt, if not outright fear. How can such people be so effective, so right so much of the time, if they can't tell you how they're doing it?

These suspicions and doubts derive from the Western tradition in philosophy which has put its entire emphasis on the rational, the systematic, the logical, the analytical, and the verbal, while consigning everything else – everything that could not be explained in words – to "lesser" realms of knowledge such as the emotions, even to the paranormal, the mystical, the magical, and the occult. However, if intuitive approaches are non-logical, and if they shun the influence of rules, how can you be taught how to use them? Can't there be a set of directions for intuitive approaches?

A set of directions or procedures is a set of rules, and the nature of intuitive approach is that it has no predetermined rules of procedure. That is why the intuitive way leads to such novel and creative results! If we followed only pre-set procedures, we'd never create anything new. The answer to this difficulty is not to search out what to do, what procedures to follow, but to discover what not to do. This is the principle of wu-wei again, of not-doing. In order to be more intuitive and more creative you must search out the obstacles of your sensitivity to your surroundings, and then systematically remove these obstacles so that the world is free to influence you. You submit yourself to the demands and conditions in the situation and allow them to have their way. Then, rather than "time" or "objectives" or "responsibilities" being managed, you will be managed…willingly, without excuses, and without needing an explanation why you are feeling good about what you are doing. The key is not, as the hippies of the 60's and 70's said, "If it feels good, do it!" The key is rather, "If it feels right, do it!" And being in, and feeling a part of, the flow of the world's conditions will feel right to you.

Some time has now passed since you completed the exercise at the beginning of this chapter. Ideally, we would prefer that you wait even longer before continuing with the second step, but if you are impatient, you may proceed. Serious initiates to the intuitive life style might prefer to wait, say, until tomorrow.

Now, without thinking about the problem or any of its details or any of the cast of characters involved, get up from where you are. Without thinking on the problem, begin an action — any action — that is related in some way — any way — to the problem. Just get up and do whatever seems to occur to you to do in that regard. Do not think about it! Do not hesitate! Just do!

There is a third step to inventorying the present: your evaluation of the effectiveness of what you've just done without thinking, formal planning, or even weighing possible consequences. Do you see something very interesting about your new action: its spontaneity, its creativity, and your comfort with it — even though it may not make sense at the level of your thinking?

What has happened? You have just behaved intuitively. That's what has happened! You have trusted your gut feelings, your instincts, and you have creatively initiated the best solution to your problem that is now available to you.

Summary

Inventorying the present is your introduction to intuitive action. It asks you to non-critically summarize as much of the current situation as you can. This summary may include the opinions of knowledgeable others regarding the situation without any attempt on your part to organize, systematize, rank, rate, or weigh any part of the situation. You let the situation's demands and conditions, past and present, do that for you without your explicitly trying to intervene or influence what is included.

Then, after some period of time, when the situation "tells you to," you will find yourself acting intuitively. Eventually, with practice, it will happen as a habit automatically, and you'll trust it.

CHAPTER FOUR

The Impartial Universe

"All things come alike to all:
there is one event to the righteous, and to the wicked."

Ecclesiastes 9:2

"the snow doesn't give a soft, white damn whom it touches."

e. e. cummings

"To understand all is to forgive all."

French proverb

We humans are a part of Nature. Its principles are our principles. We may understand some of them, but we cannot resist them. Both the physicist and the physiologist may comprehend the Law of Gravity and the consequences of a long fall, but that knowledge will not protect either of them if they jump from a tall building.

What is more important though, even when we do not grasp Nature's principles, we can still become one with them – we can go with their flow. How this is achieved we will get to later. Now we will examine what happens when we, intentionally or through ignorance, resist them. What happens is what has come to be called stress.

In social conversation, and in self-help books, no word is seen as frequently as the word stress. Everyone, for at least some part of every day, claims to be under stress, over-stressed, or stressed out. Stress is seen as the bane of our post-industrial existence, implicated in any number of diseases.

What is stress? How you answer this question is crucial because the answer will determine whether you see yourself as being able to deal with stress, and how you go about dealing with it.

Stress is a word usually given to certain bodily reactions, usually those reactions controlled through our autonomic nervous system. These include heart rate, rate and depth of breathing, facial flushing, sweating, and the secretions of certain organs and glands such as the pancreas, liver, and adrenals. They are the body's departure from equilibrium, its reaction to abrupt changes in the environment, changes which may be seen as dangerous or threatening.

When these organs and glands are overexercised, their normal, beneficial effect on the body, enabling it to deal with the environmental change, is distorted and, in time, can bring about harm, such as in chronic high blood pressure, stomach ulcers, chronic headaches, skin eruptions, and perhaps also — through the not yet clearly understood depression of our immuno-mechanisms — cancer.

The first point to keep in mind, though, is that stress consists of the distorted action of your internal mechanisms; the stress is inside you, and not in the environmental events which appear to have caused it. Your being stressed, having a headache, lower back pain, indigestion, is certainly related to some environmental event, but it is your reaction to that event which constitutes the stress. But there is more to stress than these autonomically-mediated reactions. In a very real sense, you can choose to be stressed. And you can choose not to be. How is this possible?

First, consider that the same catastrophic event will not bring about the same symptoms in everyone affected. Some will later develop headaches, others lower back pain, yet others will have nightmares, while still others will develop no symptoms at all. Not only are our reactions different from each other in response to similar events but, more important, some events are seen by certain people as not "stressful" at all. Not everyone who was in Viet Nam and saw the cruelty and devastation developed Post-Traumatic Stress Syndrome — nor did every concentration camp survivor.

Psychologists have composed lists of "stressors" with such events as divorce or the death of a loved one rated highest on the list; a serious automobile accident, being fired, or the birth of a child, a little lower down; and a minor traffic ticket near the bottom, that is, the least stressful. Such lists, however, overlook the point being made here: how a particular event is seen by an individual will influence where, or even if, it appears on that individual's list of stressors. A building collapses in Kansas City; an aircraft crashes into a hotel lobby in Indianapolis; crops fail in the Ukraine; a devastating earthquake wipes out entire cities in Soviet Armenia; there are droughts in Somalia; and hailstorms, floods, hurricanes, tornadoes, and landslides occur regularly all over, in addition to the man-made destroyers such as forced-labor camps, taxation, inflation, discrimination, and the blighting of the lives of innocent people every day by drunk drivers. None of these, however, constitutes stress. The stress is our reaction as individuals to the hailstorms, taxation, and inflation.

Why is it that the stress felt by the victims of tornadoes appears to have little correlation with the physical and financial devastation sustained? Some people who have lost everything, dear ones included, seem to bounce back, while others, who have lost little comparatively, feel stress for years. The difference between these two kinds of people is that the first kind have to deal with their horrendous loss, while the second have to deal in addition with the stress imposed by rules which have, perhaps from their earliest childhood, told them repeatedly that such catastrophies were either not supposed to happen to them, or that they were going to happen and people just had to suffer through them. People are stressed by hurricane damage not only because of the loss itself, but because their rules told them that such things weren't supposed to happen either in this particular location, at this particular time or, most important, to people who have worked so hard for so long to earn what they have.

Many of the rules you embrace, whether you are aware of it or not, are at least a potential cause of stress, a potential cause of the overexercise of your body's autonomically-mediated mechanisms. Every such rule can act to prevent you from dealing effectively (that is, intuitively) with abrupt changes in your world. When, for example, you begin to look ahead to your enjoyment of the grandchildren expected to come out of the marriage planned by your son, only to have those hopes and dreams dashed by the young man's accidental death, it is the very dreams of those fictitious grandchildren (which "ought to have been born") that will make dealing with the tragedy so much more difficult. It is the real son who was lost, not the fictitious grandchildren. They never existed — except in your rules.

Every rule, expectation, plan, goal, hope, wish and promise, every prediction, and every forecast, in some measure restricts your dealing intuitively with the circumstances of the moment. It is this restriction of your activity which overextends the normal range of activity of those internal mechanisms causing you discomfort above and beyond what those circumstances might otherwise elicit in you. The more you have invested, either emotionally or financially, in those goals, plans, and predictions, the more your actions will be restricted and the more "stress" you will feel.

It is not stress that needs to be coped with or managed, as so many books, cassette tapes, and seminars would have you believe. These commercial efforts state the problem too simply. By speaking of "stressful situations," they locate stress in the environment and, in so doing, inappropriately legitimize it. But the warm logic view is that stress is not some aspect of your world which needs to be managed. It is a part of you yourself and does not exist as such in the world around you. Neither does the management of stress (using biofeedback techniques alone) break into the stress sequence early enough. The sequence has to be short-circuited at the level of your thinking. To truly manage stress, you rid yourself of the very idea of stress, and you realize that it is people themselves who actually choose to feel stress, and to be stressed. We even choose to be angry and, worse, we focus that anger on others who "caused us" to feel angry. We blame them for how we have chosen to feel because of something they have done.

The world, however, just goes on its way according to its own principles, its own unchanging way of doing things, understood by us or not. And the people in that world do likewise. They work,

play, love, ache, and hate each in his or her own way, again understood by us or not. The world does not stress you. You do not have
to learn to cope with or to manage those events that you have decided *do* stress you. You stress yourself, and that stress represents
your overall attitude towards the world, your entire philosophy of
life. It is that philosophy, that overriding approach to living,
which changes as you allow yourself – as you dare – to become
more intuitive.

In the way they talk about anger, the French actually teach us
how better to approach this question of stress. They do not say, as
we do in English, "I'm getting angry," or, "You're making me
angry." They say, rather, *Je me mets en colere:* "I am putting myself
into anger;" that is, "I am making myself angry."

People stress themselves even in the way they attempt to "manage" their stress. Jogging, for example, so much touted as a technique
for stress management, can be a source of stress when it becomes a
device for competition against standards – any standards: you are
"trying to do what you should." That may be fine for those athletes
engaged in actual competition, but people in increasing numbers
are seeking the care of orthopedists to treat their shinsplints and
twisted ankles resulting from striving after "shoulds."

Now that we have discussed where stress is and is not located,
let us examine the roles people play in your life as "stressors."

First, an exercise. This one is called, "The Person You Hate the
Most." It is quite simple to perform, though you may find it pain-
ful, but please do it anyway; it is vital to your growth and change
as you proceed through this book.

We want you to identify the person whom you hate, despise or
resent more than anyone else, the person you hold most in contempt, perhaps because this individual has hurt you, caused you
great pain or suffering, or has otherwise made your life miserable,
preferably over a long period of time. It would be better for the
purpose of this exercise if the person were still living; however, a
deceased person will suffice, but only if no one living qualifies.

Now, think in as much detail as you can of what you know
of this person. Be systematic and orderly. Start with his or her

birthplace and early upbringing; go on to school experiences that you know about or can reasonably surmise; continue with cultural and geographic influences on the person's life; what you know about the person's family; the parents' occupation; the general economic conditions under which the person was raised; later educational experiences; travel; employment experiences — all leading up to the moment that the person did the thing that caused you to hate him or her so much. Remember, be as detailed and as accurate as you can. When you have finished, hold your thoughts, and then relate them to the information in the following pages.

When our lives are governed by rational decisions, analyses, and rules, we tend to divide people into two groups: those whose actions seem to be governed by the same set of rules as ours, and those whose actions are governed by a different set. People who obey the same rules as we do are people who do what they should. People who obey different rules from ours do not do what they should. And, while these people (and there are so many of them, aren't there?) may no longer be called heretic, evil, reprobate, or even just weird, they aren't as good as we are.

Rules, in other words, lead us to impute moral qualities and judgements to our actions and those of other people. We come to see others' actions toward us as intentionally calculated to hurt us. First, we see their actions as bad, and then we see the badness in the people themselves. We classify humanity as either friend or foe.

You have seen, through the exercise just completed, that people's lives unfold without any such notions of goodness or evil. In the history of the person you hate the most, you may have thought of a rule he or she appeared to be obeying. But did you follow that with your saying it was a good or a bad rule, or that it had good or bad consequences? We doubt it. Neither rules nor consequences are good or bad. There are just rules, and there are just consequences.

This person whom you hate so much just lived his or her life pretty much as you have lived yours. But for some reason you and that person came into conflict, and that conflict resulted in a terrible, unforgettable hurt, certainly to you, perhaps to the other person as well. But you can now see that the person you hate the most acted toward you based entirely on his or her own past. What happened between the two of you could not have happened any other way given the ways you both experienced life.

If we have a dog that keeps us awake half the night with barking, perhaps at a beetle, does that make him a bad dog? If we have a cat who knocks over and breaks a treasured vase, does that make him a bad cat? No, it does not. The barking dog and the vase-breaking cat are not bad, despite our being hurt in some way by them. They are only a cat and a dog behaving according to their nature.

In the same way, people who hurt us are not bad; they are only people. The badness in their behavior is added on by us; it is not an integral part of their actions, as is the movement of their arms or legs. People who do others harm are no different from our vase-breaking cat. Goodness and badness, and should and ought, and all the myriad of terms in our language which describe the moral dimension, are added on to people's actions by observers.

Human beings are, however, as we stated earlier, a part of Nature. We are intimately bound to it, a functioning part of it, along with every other animal, bird, and fish. Despite assertions from our biblical past that we are somehow above Nature and that we have dominion over the beasts of the field, we have, with increasing dismay over the past thirty or forty years, seen the consequences of that view in the pollution of our world and in the extinction, or near-extinction, of large numbers of animal species. There is an increasing realization that we are not above our brother and sister creatures, that we, like they, are born, grow, procreate, hunger, thirst, ache, perhaps even want and love, and certainly die. And not one of us can stand above and apart from the workings of our universe.

These workings, some thought by us to be understood, others seemingly incomprehensible, are at once irresistible and impartial. The universe does not care which of us is right or wrong, good or bad, any more than the cat cares that the vase is irreplaceable. The world only reacts to what we do. It does not judge us except as it determines the adequacy of our attempts to deal with it. When we build a building, it will stand or fall based on whether the foundation is adequate, and not whether or not it is ugly, inconveniently located, or built with stolen money or slave labor.

We humans have, at least since Ancient Greece, colored human actions differently from those of the natural world and its non-human inhabitants. We have endowed our acts with a moral quality. Instead of seeing our actions describable by the same sorts of rules as those of the natural world, we have seen them additionally as good or bad. Dogs do not consider whether or not they should bark; they simply bark. And birds fly, and cats break vases, and unlike us humans, in Walt Whitman's words,

"They do not lie awake in the dark weeping for their sins;
they do not make me sick discussing their duty to God;
not one is respectable or unhappy over the whole earth."

Part of your learning to be intuitive is neither imputing motives to nor judging other people's actions towards you. Deal with their behavior exactly as it appears, and not as a departure from the way you think it ought to be. Actions are neither appropriate nor inappropriate, cruel nor kind; they are only actions. The appropriateness or goodness is added on by us.

By the same token, and important to your own intuitive process, do not blindly accept others' opinions of your actions. If you are told that you are wrong, stupid, or even bad, recognize those labels as representing someone else's estimation of what you've done, and not as an intrinsic part of your actions themselves. Your actions are not good or bad; they are just your actions. Some psychotherapists, particularly behavior therapists, recommend to victimized, invalidated, often brutalized women that they counteract statements that they are ugly, stupid, inept, and friendless by saying to themselves over and over that they are beautiful, intelligent, competent, and popular. We do not agree with this approach. We think it unwise to dodge, parry, and throw these verbal bricks back at the offender. You do not have to choose your weapon and join the fray.

Whether or not you are inept or friendless is a matter for cold logic. We think it better that you use warm logic: clear your mind of all such value-laden words. Refuse to be labelled! You are neither ugly nor beautiful, stupid nor intelligent. You are just you (and he is just him, and they are just them). The English writer, Iris Murdoch, says it this way, "A sense of value is a sense of lack, the lack of a certain completeness...If we imagine that 'the valuable' is a property of the world...we are doomed to failure and despair."

Refusing to label actions, either yours or others', can truly make you invulnerable to much of the discord and confusion which surrounds you and threatens to engulf you every day. We said a moment ago that the workings of the universe with its natural flow, far beyond even our best judgements and attempts to analyze its principles of operation, are irresistible and impartial. Not even a modern King Canute can order the tide to halt with hope of being obeyed. To alter Nature's flow, one must still recognize and cooperate with Nature's own way. Tides are controlled by the relative positions of the Sun and Moon. To halt the tide, one must first alter the positions of those heavenly bodies. Lots of luck!

To prevent or to rid yourself of stress, forgive people for your being stressed by them. Your stress has not been their fault; they have just been going about their business. You may insist that this may be good advice for the stress, pain, or injuries that we may suffer accidentally from someone else's actions, but what about people who intended to hurt you? Does forgiving still apply? We think it does. Unless you forgive freely, quickly, willingly, even automatically, without even thinking about it, it is useless as a device for purging you of your stress. If you have to think about whether to forgive someone, whether what he or she did was intentional, whether someone deserves to be forgiven by you, you are applying cold rather than warm logic. Such a rational decision could take you the rest of your life. If courtroom juries can take weeks to deliberate the intent of a defendant's act and then still harbor some doubt, can you do better yourself with considerably less information available to you?

The problem is actually not the amount of data nor even the time available to you to decide someone's intention. The problem is that intent itself is a highly dubious notion, one which philosophers have long debated. Our view is simply this: you get the idea that a person has acted to hurt you intentionally by what that person does as if in preparation, and by what that person says about what he or she wants to happen to you. These are what judges instruct juries to be sensitive to as they infer the "intent" of defendants.

What someone says is not a cause of what he or she is going to do. What someone says, just like what he or she does, is a product of that person's past experiences in similar circumstances. If you say to your companion, "I'm going out to close the car windows," and then you do go out and close them, your going outside was not caused by your saying that you were going to. Your going out to close the car windows probably had something to do with the threat of rain; but your saying that you were going outside had more to do with our social customs of not leaving someone's presence without making some comment why. After all, had you been alone and noticed the build-up of clouds, you wouldn't have said anything before going outside.

If you are hurt by a person's actions, it is because you are a part of that person's world which has, for whatever reasons, become something that she feels needs changing. That person's intent to make such changes (involving you), as inferred from her remarks, is irrelevant, and in searching for that intent, you are looking in the wrong place for reasons why she behaved towards you as she did. The place to look is in her past, as we had you do in the exercise, "The Person You Hate the Most."

When you spend time deciding whether or not you've been hurt intentionally, you stress yourself both during the time you're deciding, and then later, as you start to think about what you're going to do about the hurt. We'll have more to say about this topic later when we talk about vindication and revenge. For the moment, we'll just state our fundamental position: one of the most effective ways you can preempt stress is to forgive the universe and everyone in it for having acted impartially, that is, without motive or interest, to hurt you or anyone else.

To help you continue on your way to a more intuitive, stress-free life, here is an old lesson offered to the world thousands of years ago. What do you think was the logic behind Christ's admonition that we forgive our enemies — those people, remember, who obey different rules than we? Here's a clue: Why do you think

Jesus was able to maintain an appearance of equanimity and serenity throughout his life?

We suggest that it was precisely because He understood this simple lesson: The universe and all the people in it are impartial; it is we who judge the world as stressful. And, as long as we judge it as stressful, we'll be stressed.

Go beyond the French proverb at the beginning of this chapter, and do not wait until you understand all to forgive all; you will likely never completely understand all. Give the impartial universe its freedom to be what it is; give the people in that universe, including yourself, their freedom to be what they actually already are, and give yourself the gift of an increasingly stress-free life!

Summary

The universe is impartial; it doesn't care what we think is right or wrong, good or bad. The universe just is. As a part of that universe, we too, just are — neither right nor wrong, good nor bad.

It is our words, particularly our labels for each other, that give us the idea that aspects of the universe have value. When we resist the universe's natural and impartial flow, when we see it as something other than what it is, we stress ourselves.

Watch out for the conflict between what is and what you have been taught ought to be!

Locating stress in the environment, then trying to manage it or cope with it, falsely legitimizes it. Stress is in you — largely in the form of rules as to how the world, and the people in it, should behave. It got there because you tried to dictate to nature how it should operate.

Do not label others' actions, and do not allow yourself to be influenced by their labels of yours. Start to live a stress-free life by forgiving the world for your having accused it of stressing you — when it had no intention to do so. It simply behaved impartially.

Part 2

Arrayed against all your intuitive leanings is a whole collection of cultural practices and conventions that you have been taught to respect from the time you started school, if not before. These are the rules of the game of life as played in Western post-industrial society. They are the obstacles which you must overcome if you are going to live intuitively. In the chapters in Part 2, we expose the insidious and counterintuitive part played in your life by an orientation toward the future, by rules you have been given by others (as opposed to rules you, yourself, have derived from your own experiences), by goal-setting, by planning—both in your personal as well as your working life, and by the words you use to try to understand both yourself and what is happening around you.

CHAPTER FIVE

The Fictitious Future

"Only lie about the future."
Johnny Carson

"The only new thing is the history you don't know."
Harry S. Truman

Acting intuitively means being deeply sensitive to the important aspects of Nature's impartial workings, and ignoring the less significant aspects. The biggest category, by far, of insignificant aspects of Nature is our own talk about and our orientation to the future.

The Xerox Company recently distributed a poster depicting how the 1980s looked to people in the 1940s. It is a very "futuristic" poster, with dogs being walked by metallic robots; streamlined rockets zooming across the scene at building-top level; high-speed, ultra-clean trains (no doubt silent); and people wearing jet-powered back-packs.

The poster is not at all how the 1980s actually were. The 1980s were characterized more by energy deficits, noise, air and water pollution, epidemic venereal disease, starvation and illiteracy — even in the United States — and terrorism on an international scale, to include the random killing of innocent shoppers unfortunate enough to have purchased over-the-counter Tylenol from a poisoned batch.

Why is the future so fantastically different from the way we pictured it would be? Were we naive, ignorant, or seduced by our own dreams? Or did something go terribly wrong? Was it supposed to work out the way we thought it would, but something got stuck in the works? What is the future, anyway? The future is fiction. Let us see why.

The future seems incredibly plastic: look how easily it is changed. Simply by going or not going to some social function – or simply by saying or doing something at that function if you do go – the entire event is changed and, perhaps, the lives of everyone there. With the advent of terrorism, that future is even more "plastic" than ever (no allusion to plastique – a favorite explosive of terrorists – intended). How different would our world have been if John F. Kennedy had bent over to retrieve something he or Jackie might have dropped at the precise moment that Lee Harvey Oswald fired? What is the future? Is it anything more than an infinity of might-be's? Can the future be seen, in some way, perhaps by people with specialized training?

It appears that no one predicted in any meaningful detail the Chernobyl nuclear accident. There may have been those who suspected that such an accident could happen. A prediction of the future, to have any value for us, must include specifics such as times and dates. Even more significant is the complete failure on the part of demographers (those are the people with all the facts, figures, data, and analyses on population trends) to predict what is almost certainly the most pervasive social phenomenon of our times: the post-World War II baby boom – either its beginning or its end.

It also appears that when accurate forecasts are made, they are made by people professing no particular training, skill, or insight into situations in any general sense. These individuals simply know one particular area particularly well, so much so that what they predict ends up happening. Further, this predictive ability does not seem to generalize. A person with an uncanny ability to predict market futures in wheat may have no such ability either in silver futures or in predicting the outcome of the next Super Bowl. Indeed who, today, would dare make a money bet – a form of prediction –

on which two teams will play in the next Super Bowl? It's too soon to hazard a guess, we'd be told. We need to wait a while.

The world is unpredictable to a significant degree. This is one of the chief sources of our stress. But we must meet the world on those terms. To attempt to do otherwise is to set ourselves up, through a self-imposed rigidity, for failure to deal with it effectively and achieve some level of happiness. We cannot predict in adequate enough detail the conditions that will exist in the future to be able to lay down an explicit set of procedures for dealing with those conditions. Of course, the closer we get to a particular point in time, the better we can predict what the situation will be. For example, you can probably state with a pretty good degree of accuracy what the temperature in your living room will be five minutes from now. But how confident are you that you can make the same statement for exactly six months from now? Just think of the variables that you'd have to consider: the weather itself, the condition of your heating or cooling system, other things that might have happened with the actual structure of your home in the meantime, the presence of another person in the house then, or perhaps one person less.

Who, for example, in 1965, would have predicted that by 1985, 10% of the adult population of the United States would be classified as problem drinkers; that drug use would become a significant problem in elementary schools nationwide; that drugs would no longer be the province of the impoverished or the desperately unhappy; that marijuana would be estimated to be California's largest cash crop ($2 billion per year); that by conservative estimates there would be 1 million frequent users of hallucinogens in the U.S., 20-25 million who have tried cocaine, and 50-60 million who have tried marijuana; and that 35% of high school seniors have admitted to having used marijuana by the 9th grade, overall what the National Institute on Drug Abuse called "the highest level of illicit drug use by young people in any industrialized nation in the world?"

Who in the fifties, or even in the sixties, would have predicted that, in 1985, Japanese automobiles of the highest quality would have captured 25-30% of the American market? And, even more astonishing, who, even after the Japanese success, would have predicted that Hyundai, a South Korean automobile, would achieve in

U.S. sales in its first import year what Nissan and Toyota took five years to accomplish?

Who, even twenty years ago, would have dreamed that the finest consumer electronics in the world, as well as the finest watches, cameras, machine tools — even table chinaware — would be manufactured not in Germany, not in Switzerland, not even in the United States, and certainly not in Great Britain, but in Japan and Taiwan?

Who in 1950 would have believed that as early as 1970 we would be facing the extinction of the Bengal tiger, with the African elephant (yes, the elephant!) not far behind?

Who in 1965 would have believed that, in 1986, the issue would not be, "Should sex education be taught in high school?" but, "Should we, in order to protect the public health from AIDS, teach safe sex practices in grade school?"

And last, who even in 1960 would have believed that the *Father Knows Best* family of a wise, successful, contented, working father; a stay-at-home but happy and fulfilled-in-her-role mother; and three exemplary children would, in 1985, comprise less than 8% of all American households? That 25% of children born in 1988 would be to unwed mothers, and that the term illegitimate, as a slur, would fall out of common use? That 24% of all households would be comprised of one person living alone? That in 60% of black families, and in 20% of white families, there would be only one parent? That some epidemiologists would estimate that as many as 50% of all American adults might be carrying herpes antibodies?

We cannot see the future, at least in any of its specifics, any better now than we could, say, twenty years ago. Even those people who have premonitions, or those who continually act with what has been called insight, ESP, second sight, or clairvoyance rarely attempt predictions with any degree of specificity.

When we think about the past, we seem to see things that existed in the past. These are things we "remember" — a favorite chair, for example. Sometimes these things still exist. We see them now, and we remember them as they were. We say that their existence continues from the past into the present. Some people have also suggested that our chair's existence, as well as our own existence, will continue unbroken into the future. So, when people think about the future, they see themselves there, and a favorite chair as well. When people think in this fashion, it is easy for them to believe that, in some way, the future chair, as part of the future as a whole, already exists as a sort of pre-existing shadow, much as some believe that the past continues to exist in our memories. That is, the future is of the same kind of reality as the past, a mirror image of the time-dimensional aspect of the past.

Some people do claim to be able to see this future. Let us examine this for a moment. In order for someone to actually see the future, there must first be a future to be seen, a perpetual shadow-play in hyperspace, in advance of the real thing accessible only to certain specially gifted people.

But wait! Wouldn't there be many, many such shadow-plays going on, simultaneously, depending on which one one wanted to access, occurring in intervals of time ahead of the present moment? There would be one shadow-play for five minutes ahead, another for, say, fifteen minutes, then thirty minutes, one hour, one day, one week, and so on, rather like there seems to be in our memories many past events corresponding to intervals in our lives gone by. That is, some people claim to be able to see the future at a specified distance rather like we all seem able to "replay" in our memories the events of last year or of five years ago. In addition, these people claim to be able to make accurate predictions of the outcome of our present actions.

Our view is that while they may intuitively sense a direction in which to move, they do not see an outcome. No one specific thing or person actually exists in any way in the future. What then does exist there? What gives the future its form and character? The answer is that nothing exists in the future. Nothing is fore-ordained. The future is a fiction, and when people say that they see the future, no actual seeing is going on. What is happening is the envisioning by people of what they think should or ought to happen.

The difficulty of predicting the future is why such advice as that given in the book, *How You Can Find Happiness During the Collapse of Western Civilization*, is useless: "By the right thing, I am referring to the action that, at any given time, will bring you the greatest long-term success." The author, Robert Ringer, unfortunately does not tell us how we can possibly know what will bring us the greatest long-term success at any point in time. Mr. Ringer also suggests that in deciding what you want out of life, you first need to determine what the costs are of obtaining those things. But he does not tell us how to determine what the costs are going to be. The reason why he does not tell us is because he cannot. No one can foresee all the consequences of his or her behavior. As we will point out throughout this book, the basis for your actions must lie elsewhere from your "guess-timations" of what the future holds.

The future, as we have just said, is a fiction. It certainly does not exist now, if only by its very definition. And, in terms of the details we need in order to plan for it, it will not exist then. The future cannot be seen because it is not there to be seen, and talking at any length about it, or planning systematically for it without at least building in a lot of flexibility to handle the changes that will inevitably occur, is the worst sort of time management. It is time wasted.

Another book currently for sale on bookstore racks is titled, *What to Do with the Rest of Your Life*. It is a book on career planning, and the title certainly sounds harmless enough. Indeed it incorporates a noble sentiment in our culture, that one's life should be planned. But wait a minute! Just what is the rest of your life? If the future is a fiction, then is that not also true of your personal future? Is the rest of your life also a fiction?

We will begin to answer that question by answering another one first. First, we will answer the question, "Why is it a good idea to keep asking yourself, 'What is the best thing for me to be doing right now?'" This is the question asked by Alan Lakein in his bestselling book in the field of time management, *How to Get Control of Your Time and Your Life*. When you do not do something that is best done now, you set up a situation in which you are tense and apprehensive. You ruminate constantly about all those things that need doing: when will you have time for this, or for that?

You become what Richard B. Wright called a "weekend man," a person who has abandoned the present in favor of what happened in the past or what may happen, perhaps what he hopes will happen, in the future. Such a person, instead of living and acting in the present, spends most of the time – and most of his or her thoughts – in a preoccupation with the future, with all the things that need to be done, but never actually getting started on them. That person becomes more and more miserable, desperate, and impotent.

The corporate equivalent of the weekend man is remarkably prevalent in the world of work today. This is the organization executive whose meetings, retreats, and planning seminars abandon the present in favor of the past ("Why did we fail to predict the October 19, 1987 crash?"), or of the future ("What should our goals and objectives be for the next three years?"). This sort of thinking is so pervasive in our society, and so misguided, that we have devoted several chapters to exposing its flaws and the part it plays in stressing our lives. We are referring, of course, to goal setting and planning.

The reason why we are advised by these experts on time management to do it now, is that this is the only time we have. The past is already gone. You cannot take advantage of circumstances that no longer exist. For example, you cannot buy at the former price, a stock which used to be at 12-1/4 but is now at 37-1/2. Likewise, you cannot sell a stock you now own, at its former price of 38-1/2 when it is now selling at 16-1/2. You only add to your misery when you agonize over the "missed" opportunities. The future, on the other hand, is not yet here, and it may never arrive – for you. In *Journey to Ixtlan*, Carlos Castaneda relates how annoyed his tutor and friend, the Yaqui Indian Don Juan, became when Castaneda's attitude toward life was not changing as a result of their shared experiences. The Indian accused Castaneda of thinking he had plenty of time to change but, on the contrary, Don Juan pointed out that any particular act might just be the very last. He went on to point out that there is no individual or agency anywhere who would guarantee that any of us will live until tomorrow morning. Your personal future, as you envision its details, is only a fiction. Right now is when you must fix the hole in the screen door, patch the hole in the driveway, call Aunt Mary, buy the birthday gift, make an appointment with your accountant or physician, because right now is when the contingencies prompting those actions are operating on you. They were not operating yesterday (or you would have "felt the urge" to do those things yesterday). And they may not operate on you so strongly tomorrow (other contingencies may have overwhelmed them). As the Greek Epictetus said, "Do you know that disease and death must needs overtake us, no matter what we are doing? ...What do you wish to be doing when it overtakes you? ...If you have anything better to be doing when you are so overtaken, get to work on that."

When you consider just how much your worrying about the future contributes to your stress level, you can see that living in the present can eliminate an incredible amount of stress before it even starts. For example, when your mate sees the dented car fender; or when a particular situation materializes at work tomorrow (keeping you awake half the night), all the fears of what will happen will disappear in a flash, and take your stress with it, if you are prepared simply to wait and deal with these events after they have occurred. Much of the energy that would otherwise go into your apprehension can be used to deal with what really is happening now.

Whether you'll have time to do one thing or another, or worrying about what someone may do can so paralyze you that things occurring now are not dealt with, or are dealt with only superficially, thus compounding your anxiety and making the situation even worse. It can do you no good, and perhaps much harm, for you to worry about the lump in your breast, or the pain in your chest, before the test reports come in and are interpreted by your physician.

Deal with the now! How foolish you will feel when all your worry, concern, and stress have been for nothing — when the lump in your breast turns out to be a blocked milk duct, and the pain in your chest turns out to be indigestion. Actually, worrying about the future may contribute as much as anything else to the symptoms of chronic heart disease.

Logan Wright, former president of the American Psychological Association, said that "time urgency" is one of three components of "Type A personality" — the type highly vulnerable to heart attack.

Statements made by physicians to cancer patients, for example, that they have "only 6 months to live" now take on a somewhat different meaning. If only we could be guaranteed that we had as much as 6 months to live! Such predictions by physicians are not so terrifying when you consider that, in those words of Don Juan, not one person or agency in the entire world is prepared to guarantee that you will live even until midnight tonight.

Why risk all that wear and tear on your body for something that may never come to pass? Stress, as we have already seen, is not something in your environment impacting on you. Nature is impartial. The stress is a reaction in you. But if you live now, if you recognize that you cannot deal with the future now, if you recognize that everything you've worried about hasn't happened, and may not happen at all, you can begin to lead a largely stress-free life. Attempting to deal with the future now will cause you only anxiety, apprehension, and worry.

As we just suggested by our "Who would have predicted?" items, not only can you not predict the future in any meaningful way, but having done so sets you up for terrible disappointments, disorientation, and dismay when something entirely different happens.

Looking ahead, having a vision of what you want to achieve, and seeing your goals clearly, are all ways in which our western culture has taught us to label certain kinds of private experiences. In the same way, dreaming, imagining — even thinking — are labels which our culture, starting with our parents, then later our teachers and colleagues, taught us to use to talk about our private lives. When we talk to friends about our having dreamed or vividly imagined that we were driving a particular car, and that we had eventually acquired such a car, our friends might have told us that in so doing we'd seen our goal clearly, perhaps even seen the future.

But what had we actually seen? If we restrict our use of the word "see" to those situations where our retinas are changed by something in our environment, with a consequent firing of the optic nerve, then it is clear that envisioning our goals does not involve actually seeing anything. At best, that sort of seeing is metaphorical, and there is nothing at all wrong with such a metaphor so long as we keep its figurative use in mind.

We create a lot of difficulties for ourselves when we do not keep that figurative use in mind. We begin to see the future, particularly those parts of it that interest us — such as our goals — as existing in some sort of hyperspace, not existing yet, but waiting to exist, waiting to happen. Further, we start to believe the statements of certain people such as psychics who claim, through some sort of second sight, to be able to see this future which is waiting to happen and to make statements (predictions) about it. But what is happening is that they are not seeing the future; their "seeing" is not the same sort of seeing as our looking outside and seeing a holly bush. Their seeing is metaphor. They are, though, precisely through being intuitive, very accurate in their predictions.

An application of this "predictive" aspect of warm logic has been called creative-visualization. In this technique the individual imagines as intensely and in as much detail as possible those things, events, states of affairs, etc., as he or she wishes them to be. People claim that by so doing, they make these events more likely to happen. Is this occult and magical thinking or is there really something going on here?

We have just pointed out that when you imagine something, you are not actually seeing anything. There is nothing out there in some other dimension which is being contacted. What is happening is an intensive experiencing of something without that something being present. But, you may ask, granting that such an experience can occur, how can it bring something into being?

If you simply visualize, say, a vacation in the Yorkshire Dales in the north of England, then it is likely that nothing further will come of the experience. But let us suppose that you attempt to make the experience much more vivid and accurate in all its details. You would, in order to be able to do that, have to peruse travelogues, look at maps, read one or two of John Herriott's books, as well as perhaps those of the Bronte sisters. Your creative visualizations would thereby become clearer. But you could do even more. You might start a subscription to *The Yorkshire Post*, write letters to people operating bed-and-breakfast establishments in Harrogate, and arrange to listen to the British Broadcasting Corporation's Overseas Service for news of the area.

Now your creative visualization would be truly more vivid and accurate. But you still have further to go. A vacation in the Dales requires that you have a passport. You must visualize that too, as well as the application you must fill out in order to obtain one; the check you must write; the passport photograph of yourself that must accompany the application; and all the things one must do in order to have money to buy the airline ticket.

You can now see how creative visualization can actually bring something like a vacation into existence. It does this not by some magical wand-waving, but by itself constituting a good part of what needs to be done in every ordinary way to have a vacation. Creative visualization is nothing more nor less than what everyone does who envisions what they think they want, and then acts to obtain it.

A list of things to be done, however, is not a "plan." It is, rather, a set of prompts which functions as a technique of self-control to move your actions in the direction of creating what you want. You can't help but achieve what you want, the more intensely and vividly you visualize what it is that you want — that situation in which you'd be happiest. The most intense visualization of a passport requires that you have one in front of you. And the most intense visualization of your passport requires that you have yours in front of you.

There is another sort of visualization which is beginning to receive some publicity in homeopathic medicine circles: the use during cancer treatment of techniques by which the sick person is encouraged to imagine healthy cells in his or her body attacking and eliminating the maldeveloped cells of the tumor. Such visualization has been followed in several cases by a remission of symptoms. It must be kept in mind, though, that whatever has caused these remissions may have only the most indirect link with the patient's visual imagery itself. It is more likely that various bodily processes such as hormone secretions, changes in respiration, and metabolic alterations, which can now be spoken of in only the most circumspect way, accompany the patient's visualizing a cellular battle; and it is these bodily processes which are responsible for the improvement in the patient's condition.

The reasons for the widespread belief in the reality of the future may rest in our Western Christian views of the afterlife. The afterlife is in some sense the future, and it waits for us (Death is "He Who Waits") as the eventual reward or punishment for our activities here on Earth. Our Western religious orientation teaches us to try to control this future after we are dead by exhorting us to work to achieve life everlasting in Heaven, and it is only a short step from there for us to try to control a future which is presumed to exist in some way before we die.

Another part of the reason for our belief that the future is out there waiting to happen is the view popular with most linguists that our language is "about things;" that is, our language refers to things. At a simple level this common-sense view causes us little trouble. Our word cat seems quite adequate in enabling us to handle all of our dealings with the charming furry thing that lives with us. But the issue gets a little more complicated when we talk about things that are not now present to our sight or touch, and maybe never will be, such as unicorns and dragons. How can we say that our words about the future refer to things in the future when that future neither exists now nor perhaps ever will? Actually, words come tumbling out of our mouths in long chains, and there is no necessary connection between those words and events and things in the present and past. And there is certainly none between those words and the future simply because there can be no such reference. There is no thing to which to refer.

"Not so fast!" you may say. "The referent is, in the case of the future, imagined." And that is exactly the point! The future is entirely imagined. This idea is not so far-fetched. The language of the Hopi Indians of the American Southwest has no sense of time the way we think of it. There is instead a differentiation of everything into two realms: everything now existing in the present along with everything that has occurred in the past. These two spheres are spoken of in the same way, as though they were equivalent realities.

On the other hand there is, indistinguishable from one another, everything that we Westerners think of as the mental as well as what we think of as the future. That is, the mental and the future are spoken of in the same way, as though they are equivalent realities in a separate realm.

The Hopis understand the future entirely as metaphor, and they place the future completely within the realm of the mental and the imaginary, and not, as we do in the Greek-Christian West, in the same realm as the past and the present. The Hopi view is no different from the concept of the future presented throughout this chapter: the future exists only in our heads. Hence words cannot "refer" to it, or be "about it."

One interesting practical application follows from this view of the future: in living the intuitive lifestyle one can never make a mistake.

What is a mistake? It is a label we pin on something we've done when we later realize that certain unfortunate consequences resulted from that action. Examples are playing a high card in bridge and having it trumped, or moving the king's rook on the chessboard and having it immediately taken by an unnoticed pawn, or taking one freeway exit instead of another only to find out ten miles later that it was the "wrong" one; all mistakes.

The important word in the last paragraph is "later." You can only know later that a particular action was a mistake. But at the very moment that the action takes place, how can you know? If you knew, you wouldn't have done it. If you had been sensitive to all the possibilities in the situation, you would have done something else. You would have played a different card, moved another chess piece, or taken a different freeway exit. But you weren't sensitive to the entire gamut of possibilities, and you didn't. It was only later that you decided you were wrong.

What this means is that when you live in the present, in the here and now, no action you ever take can be seen as a mistake. Of course, hindsight is always 20-20. Mistakes are always judgements, yours or someone else's, of your own actions after the fact. But your action is taking place now, in the present. You cannot expect to be able to judge your current actions with information you can't possibly have until later. And do not let others judge your present actions with information they'll also have to wait to receive, either.

No action has any sort of "meaning" or value except after-the-fact. Then, that "meaning" is added on separately and artificially, and is always subject to change. This is why ethicists who claim that the moral value of actions lies in their consequences don't help us judge the wisdom of our acts now. Right now we don't know what the consequences of our actions are going to be. We can only guess based on what has happened in similar situations.

Gregory Bateson, the brilliant ethnologist and communications theorist, said in his *Steps to an Ecology of Mind* that the value of an act must be "implicit and simultaneous with the act itself, not separate from it in the sense that the act would derive its value from reference to a future end or goal." The only way you can achieve this implicitness and simultaneity is by not thinking about the possible consequences of the particular act you are contemplating. That the act will have consequences, you may be sure, but what value they will give to the act must remain to be seen. How often have you thought of the happy accident that brought you and a close friend or mate together? Haven't you speculated that if you hadn't gone to that particular school, taken that particular job, spent that particular vacation, or even gone to the supermarket on that special day, you would never have met that special someone, and your life would not have taken that new turn?

But all of this was unknown at that time you enrolled at that school, took that job – and even now you do not know the end of the story. That fateful meeting could turn out to have a still different meaning to you if the relationship sours. All of which is to say, not only is there is no such thing as a mistake, but also you can change your past. You cannot, of course, change what has actually happened, but you can change the importance of any event or action in your past simply by what you do in the present. You can make it very important, or you can make it irrelevant. Perhaps this is what Henry Ford meant when he said, "All history is bunk!"

What about the much-recommended "taking the long view" of things? By all means you are most likely to benefit from taking the long view – but understand that we mean by this the long view back through the past, not into the future. When someone is "short-sighted," he or she is failing to consider not what the future may bring, but what has happened in the past. Such a long view of the past will protect you, as much as it is possible to be protected in this uncertain world, from the undesirable and unhealthy long-term consequences of actions which in the short term may be pleasurable. The more you are sensitive to the long-term consequences in your and your acquaintances' pasts, as they are now making themselves felt, of smoking, poor diet, lack of exercise, drug use, sexual promiscuity, or treating people in general with contempt or suspicion, the more protected you will be as you act in the present.

When you live in the present, you become immediately free of the stress brought on by self-recriminations over the past, since you have never made a mistake. And you are immediately free of the stress brought on by worries over the future, worries about unfinished business, unsettled conflicts, unattained goals, and unfulfilled promises to yourself or to others.

Summary

Much of our stress comes from worrying about the future — worrying about what is going to happen. If we could only know! We even pay people to try to see, predict, or foretell the future — from economic forecasters to seers and mystics.

When making a choice of actions, you can't foresee all the consequences and, to be intuitive, you must stop trying to. Any attempt to describe the future, particularly your own future, is futile. It becomes stressful when things don't turn out the way you thought they would, and such attempts prevent you from enjoying life's surprises. Much of your current stress may come from thinking that things were supposed to have worked out differently from the way they are now.

The future is not "out there" waiting to happen. It exists only in your imagination as a fiction. It cannot be described, and it is, therefore, a most unreliable basis for your actions now.

The future is almost infinitely plastic and changeable – by you! Mistakes are impossible, because you can't ever know at the moment an action is taken what the consequences (which you will then evaluate) are going to be.

CHAPTER SIX

Filtering the World: Rules

"Any fool can make a rule."

Henry David Thoreau

"In the world of mules there are no rules."

Ogden Nash

From the time in your early childhood when your parents first suspected that you could understand, they stopped telling you just to do things like, "Sit down!" or "Don't touch that!", and they started to instruct you to do things, or not to do things, because certain things "are so." Eventually, as you grew up, all your actions became justifiable to your parents on the basis of these reasons. Whenever you tried to worm out of a chore around the house, mother said, "Because I'm your mother, and I said so!", or, "Because if the trash isn't taken out, there'll be flies all over the house," or, "Because if you don't get the groceries now, you won't have them for the barbecue tomorrow," or, "Because kids are supposed to do household chores."

Think back...if mother asked why you had done something which she disapproved, she expected an answer in the same terms as those she had given earlier, when she had told you why you had to do something. If you were taught that disobedience to parents was due to being tempted by the devil, you were expected to explain your own misconduct in those terms. If you ever gave another kind of explanation, such as, "Well, Mom, I think that talking with Nancy about rock stars is more important than household chores," or "I just felt like it," or, "I don't know," then you received, at the very least, a quizzical look or, more likely, a strong verbal response which may have also included a certain amount of physical violence or deprivation of privilege.

In this way, as you grew into adulthood, you were taught to think about, justify, and explain your actions. These statements of explanation and justification are called rules. They are the way you were taught to think the world works and, therefore, by implication, how you should act in that world.

Some rules you yourself derived from your own experiences. These tended to change as new experiences dictated, and they are, therefore, not much of a problem to you. If you are asked, by someone who is watching you wax your cross-country skis, why you are using blue wax rather than green, and you tell that person how you determined the temperature of the snow, that answer is based on your past experience, and perhaps also on your having read a book on how to wax skis. If you are asked why you are planting tomatoes in a certain way, or why you have put scallions between your rose bushes, your reply, again, is likely to be based on either or both your past experiences, and your having read about how to protect roses from aphids. These are called derived rules.

Derived rules — those you have derived by yourself from your own experiences — do not create stress for you. Being obtained from experience, they can be readily changed as new experiences dictate, and are not likely to get you into trouble when something unexpected comes along. You just incorporate that event into a fund of experiences from which your intuitive capabilities stem, and you go on from there. If your rule for preparing poached trout is to let the fish sit in simmering water for eight minutes for each inch of the fish's diameter, and you find, at an altitude of 7,000 feet, that the fish remains raw, you don't hesitate to change your rule to nine or ten minutes. Also, rules derived from experience aren't likely to tell you what ought to happen, just what does happen when you yourself act in certain ways.

There is another kind of rule, however, which was also given to you as a child, usually by your parent or another adult, or perhaps found in a book, which has probably not been modified by your experiences. These rules are universal statements of should, ought, or supposed to, and we call them given rules. Here are some examples.

If you are asked why you don't quit your rat-race job and buy that antique shop you've often spoken of, and you answer, "Because you should be prepared to sacrifice job satisfaction now for good retirement benefits later," you are offering a universal "should" or "ought to" as a rationale for your behavior. And, if you are asked why, now that you are within three months of your thirtieth birthday, you are so depressed, and you answer, "Because I should be married by now," you are again giving a universal should or ought to as a reason, this time for your feelings.

It does not matter whether or not your should's or ought to's are based on scientifically accurate data; that is, whether the rule you give is indeed the actual, verifiable reason for your actions. In fact, usually, such rules cannot be validated or invalidated by data. All that is important is whether the reason you give, either straight out or with minimal prompting, is a universal statement of should or ought to. To the extent that continued prompting cannot get you to give your reason for action (or inaction) in terms of a should or ought, you may be acting intuitively...which is good! Your answers, your rules, are the device by which you have put evaluative labels on your — and others' — actions. And that's where the trouble begins. That is the place where stress is created.

We have listed below several rules which many people have been taught to give as reasons for their actions.

1. You should live your life according to generally accepted rules.
2. You should plan so that you can achieve long-range goals.
3. You should get what you deserve.
4. You should avoid mistakes.
5. You shouldn't want things that are bad for you.
6. You should try to live up to other people's expectations.

7. You should care how people will remember you.
8. You should always honor your commitments and keep your promises.

There are many, many such rules. Some are widespread within a culture, while others are found only in particular families, geographic regions, or religious groups. Think for example how you would complete each of the following sentences, so that each one would then form a given rule, depending on whether you were a female Hispanic-American, a male middle-class Black, second-generation Norwegian, Tennessee working-class, a male blue-collar Irish-American, a female Italian-American professional, a male Italian-American professional, California Jewish, New Jersey Jewish, New Mexico pueblo Native American, or old-money Eastern Establishment:

> Mothers ought (not)...
> Grandparents ought (not)...
> Women should (not)...
> A son should (not)...
> A daughter-in-law should (not)...
> A marriage ought (not)...
> Children of divorce should (not)...
> Money should (not)...

All such rules governing the actions of someone of your gender, age, ethnic group, and economic class were already in place when you were born, ready and waiting for you, all of them presented to you, sooner or later, as universal unqualified directives. As such, certainly some have come to hamper your ability to deal with the world, because they intervene between you and it. One or more of the rules above, or others similar to them, may be the basis for your inability to solve the problem you wrote down in the exercise at the beginning of Chapter 3, Inventorying the Present. Is this a rule which you must now modify or violate in order for you to make progress on the problem; the rule which says you can't or shouldn't do whatever needs to be done in order to solve the difficulty? Write down a rule that is a universal statement of should or ought which seems to govern your actions with regard to the problem you listed.

Now can you see why your problem has been so intractable? It is because its solution requires that you violate one of your given rules.

Sometimes the impact of given rules on your life is made even more obscure and insidious by somebody's first making equivalent for you things that otherwise might be seen as different. The unemployed woman trying to find work who was taught as a child, "Exercise is recreation and, if you're out of work, you shouldn't spend time doing it," may find herself unable to participate in her usual aerobic fitness program. The man trying to keep his weight down who was taught as a child, "Food is scarce, and you should never waste it," may find it impossible when food is plentiful not to eat the food left in the serving platters or in the cooking pots after everyone at the table, including himself, has eaten their fill.

The most insidious shoulds of all are those telling you how you should feel in particular situations: how you should feel on the death of a loved one, on the winning of a prize, on the birth of a child, on the loss of a contract bid, on having gotten divorced, on having discovered your child is on drugs, or on having gotten fired. These shoulds are dangerous in the extreme; they invalidate you at the most private and personal level. How you should feel is how you do feel. That others might feel different is only a statement of human differences, not that you are somehow wrong, abnormal, or perverse for not feeling as they would.

Much of this book is devoted to calling into question these universal rules which masquerade as essential guides to dealing with the world, but which actually prevent us from achieving both success and happiness in such dealings. Some of these universal statements of should and ought we'll deal with specifically; others, we'll deal with indirectly. But throughout this book it is our contention that people who offer as reasons for their actions such rules as we have listed are very likely to be unhappy, unfulfilled, oppressed, depressed, confused, dependent, anxious, frustrated, and guilt-ridden. These people are also likely to be merely tolerated by their acquaintances and generally held in contempt and victimized.

Those words "should," "ought to," or "supposed to" always hide someone's desire to preempt our wishes and preferences. After all, we all have our own ideas about the way things ought to be. So whose ideas should be adopted, mine or yours? Does it make any difference whether someone says, "Do it this way because it is what I want," or, "Do it this way because that's the way it's supposed to be"? Of course it makes a difference! You are more likely to conform to the person's request if it is stated the second way. When parents say to their children that they ought to behave a certain way, they think they are more likely to be obeyed than if they said, "Do it because I said so!"

You may have purchased this book because you hoped it would help you deal with your unhappiness, depression, or confusion, or that it might help you understand why you have vague medical symptoms such as headaches or rashes which you have been told are psychological in nature. If you have been candid in assessing your compliance to given rules, you now understand why you have these symptoms. Confusion, depression, and many medical symptoms emerge from ongoing conflicts between what you want to do, and what you feel you ought to do.

Usually what you want to do is obvious to you. You want to see this movie rather than that one; you want to eat at a particular Italian restaurant this evening rather than making something at home; you want to drink a cola rather than a lemon-lime soda pop; you want to watch Monday-night football instead of going bowling. Sometimes, though, you're not sure what you want. You vacillate. You're confused.

When the vacillation is just a question of seeing one movie or another, it is not important; you can always see one of the films tonight, and catch the other some other time. But when the uncertainty deals with whether or not to divorce Mary or whether or not to tell your boss to go to hell, you must tread carefully. Can you know whether you've made the right move? Is there in such important life decisions even such a thing as the right or the wrong move?

There is a right move in these matters for you. It is that action which is followed by the disappearance of the confusion, depression, headaches, nightmares. But how do you get there? Most people are not able to say clearly what they want. What you say you want is very likely bound up tightly with what you've been taught to think you ought to have. The following technique will help you put what you want into words. When you have learned to trust your own warm logic, it may not matter to you that you can't always "say what you want."

Pick someone you respect, who knows you well, and in whose interest it is to tell you the truth. Close relatives, being frequently involved in the conflict you are trying to resolve, are not likely to qualify for this task. Find someone else. Then ask the person to describe, in as much detail as he or she can, the situation in which he or she thinks you'd be happiest. Have him or her include everything: the physical situation as well as the social, familial, and vocational. Caution this person not to take what you've been saying too much at face value, but to weigh your words and actions carefully. Then, listen to him or her. The components of the situation described by your friend, if he or she is at all perceptive, is a list of what you probably want.

Now that you can say what you want, try to figure out what you think you deserve, what you ought to have, what you should be doing, all of which we assume conflict with what you say you want. What you ought to have, or ought to be doing are embedded in the rules you were taught as a youth, emphasized by your parents, drummed into your head, so that you carry them around with you all the time—even now. But it is not likely that rules which come easily to mind are the ones involved in your current conflicts and the symptoms they've produced. It is the rules which are not obvious to you that you now need to discover. They are the ones causing the problems.

To discover these rules you need to find someone who not only has your respect and who tells you the truth, but someone who also has known you for a long time, someone who perhaps also knew your parents and how they raised you. This could be the same person whom you asked to tell you what you wanted. Ask this person, "What are the rules, in terms of universal should's and ought's, that I appear to be obeying as I live my life?" You might also want to add the condition that these rules might be ones you would be extremely reluctant to break.

If your friend serves you well in this exercise, you will feel a sense of recognition as the rules are revealed. You may not like hearing them (the truth does hurt, at least sometimes) but you will recognize them. Write down two or three of the most important ones you have discovered.

Now examine these given rules for current acceptability. Do you recognize where they came from, who gave them to you? Were they given to you so early in life that they were accepted quite independent of your own experiences and opportunities to judge their merit for yourself? And, have they remained unchanged even though your subsequent experiences might have changed them had you realized they were influencing you?

If these rules were indeed given to you by your parents, and your parents are now dead, the rules can have a particular potency. As long as your parents are living, you can argue these universal statements of should or ought with them, or you can put physical distance between yourself and your folks if these debates are painfully acrimonious and cannot be resolved. But after your parents are dead, no arguing the merits of the rules, and no distancing is possible. What this means is that you must not allow differences of opinion with your parents over universal statements of should or ought to persist! Resolve them now however you can!

It is important to remember that, as guides for our actions, rules are not "Right" nor are they "Wrong." Even when they are specific to situations (like protecting roses from aphids, or waxing cross-country skis) and not universal shoulds or ought to's, they are still better understood as precise but unfinished. That is, they usually do not include all the possible variations in the situations they presume to guide us through. There are always likely to be new varieties of roses which may need new and different kinds of onions to protect them from new varieties of aphids. And, in the case of statutes and ordinances, it is why legislation must be supplemented by continual litigation.

On the other hand, a non-analytic intimacy with situations is never precise in the sense that it can be reduced to a rule or an equation, but it is always complete. It always represents, as far as it goes, the most up-to-date version of your familiarity with that particular situation, and it is your best guide to what to do regarding divorce, your old car, or any other important problem. The paramount thing to keep in mind is that whether or not you can sort out all the intricacies of all the contingencies which operate daily on you, your body does it for you automatically. It is not necessary for you to be able to verbalize and analyze all the details of the world's impact on you. Your body, all that is you, is already doing it. And it is communicating its findings to you non-verbally at every waking, sleeping and dreaming moment.

Some given rule is almost certainly the source of your inability to solve the major problems in your life, whether it is, in the case of an unwanted pregnancy, that you should never even consider an abortion or, in the case of a wife's alcoholism, that one should always keep embarrassing matters like that hidden within the family. Some such given rule, some such universal statement of should or ought, is the source, or at least one of the sources, of your conflicts and the symptoms produced by them. What you were told long ago that you should do (or think, or feel) is now contrary to what your own more recent experiences would recommend. What you must now decide is the extent to which your given rules are statements of the way you want to live now. Will continuing to obey them, at least in their present form, prevent you from getting what you want? We suspect that your answer to this question is an emphatic YES!

Sensitivity to the world is achieved in good measure through the elimination of the effects of given rules on your current predicament. As these rules disappear or are modified, there is an increase in the collective effects of all the contingencies which have ever impacted on you, and a commensurate increase in your happiness and fulfilment.

Summary

Given rules prescribe behavior either for a world that has changed considerably from when you were first given them (particularly if you were born before 1970), or for a world that actually existed only in the mind of the person who gave them to you. Since those rules were given to you very early in life, you probably have been only dimly aware of them, let alone examined them for applicability to your present world. As a result, your actions have frequently been inappropriate to circumstances, inconsiderate of certain kinds of people, or just generally ineffective.

Some people have no doubt attempted subtly to correct these ineffective actions of yours. They may have looked at you disapprovingly, failed to grant your requests, or even avoided you completely. Perhaps you have been tormented by your inability to grasp why such unpleasant occurrences happened so often to you, and you may even have developed symptoms like headaches, ulcers, anxiety, and depression, all because of the hidden conflict between what you want and what some given rule told you that you should have.

It has not been our intent in this chapter that you throw out all your given rules. To figure out all of them could take years; it might even take particular situations to bring them to the surface. What you must do, though, is to look at them and evaluate them in terms of the sort of life you want to be living, but are not living now. It would help considerably if you were to add the following phrase to all your shoulds: "…according to _____'s rules." Then you'd fill in the blank with the name of the person who gave you the rule.

Some of the rules may indeed need to be discarded as the vestiges of a long-forgotten past, but others you may still value and, with or without modification, may be rules by which you still want to continue to live…at least for now.

CHAPTER SEVEN

Filtering the World: Goals

"What we call results are beginnings."

Ralph Waldo Emerson

There were many fine sports cars on the roads in the 1950s. The MG-TC was among the first of the imports from England — then almost unrivaled as a performance-automobile powerhouse. Then came the Austin Healey 1000 and the fabulous Jaguar XK-120. If you wanted something a little more expensive, there were Alfa Romeo and Morgan before you got to names like Ferrari and Maserati. There were even some interesting American marques: the first Chevy Corvette was seen in 1953, followed by Ford's Thunderbird a year or two later. But the sports car par excellence of the fifties was the Mercedes-Benz 300-SL, or its younger brother (some would have invidiously said "sister"), the 190-SL.

One of this book's authors, aged eighteen in 1956, the first production year of the 190-SL, and for whom that car was to be for years far beyond his means, said, "Someday I'm going to own that car!" Twenty-two years later, having some money available, and seeing such a car for sale, he did.

However, this is not a happy tale of a cherished goal attained, a life's ambition reached, for the story does not end here.

Over the next few years that car, despite thousands of dollars of repair and restoration, stranded the author and his wife many times on desolate back roads, at night and in the rain, and utterly failed to give him even a fraction of the pleasure he had anticipated.

What went wrong? Was it the goal statement itself; the actual achieving of it; the perhaps unrealistic expectations; this particular car; the low level of competence of the car's many mechanics; all the above; none of the above? Aren't goals supposed to be achieved? Or are they like the Holy Grail, only to be yearned after always just out of reach? What can be learned from this expensive experience in goal attainment?

The first lesson is the wisdom of the Americanism, "Be careful what you ask for; you just might get it." The chief lesson learned is this: even when your statement that you want something is what you'd actually choose and pay for, free of any pressure from given rules regarding what you should want, it can still create problems if it is too specific. Goals, especially long term goals, must be "hazy," loosely defined. And, the further in the always fictitious future your choice is likely to be made, the more hazy the goal must be.

Wouldn't it have turned out better if, instead of saying, "Someday I'm going to own that car," the author had said, "Someday I'm going to own a car, perhaps something like a 190-SL, which will excite me just like that car is doing right now?" The author's problems with the car came directly from his having stated the goal too specifically despite the actual opportunity to acquire it being years in the future. It would have been better had he said to himself, when finally confronted with the opportunity to buy the car, "Hey, wait a minute. Although I've always wanted this car, there are plenty of more recent, just-as-exciting brands, and in much better condition than this one." The goal of the Mercedes-Benz 190-SL was so specific that it had completely closed off all other options.

It is important to remember that when you establish a goal, you do not thereby create something in that nether-world called the future which will now beckon you to strive toward it. To see goals this way sets you up for frustration and disappointment as well as obstructing your choices as new circumstances require. A goal is not a "thing" at all; it is a statement you make to yourself. It is your vision of what you think you want. And, while such statements may start as descriptions of things you want, descriptions of things that you'd choose to do or to obtain now, if you had the means available, they can frequently become rules, things you ought to choose now because you promised them to yourself some time ago.

The way to prevent this from happening is to keep your goals — your statements of preference — hazy, unclear, and vague. Think of how you want to feel when you achieve them. Don't define their actual appearance. In so doing you will leave the way clear for more effective dealing with situations as they occur and for deeper feelings of achievement — which are really what goal setting is all about.

Actually, it seems that ordinary people are smarter than "the experts" in this regard since many of them do appear to live their lives without the clearly stated goals that experts insist are needed in order to be happy and fulfilled. Ordinary people appear to recognize the dangers of setting explicit goals. Here are five possible reasons for your not setting them:

1. You might be setting up the possibility of failure; without goals, there can be no possibility of failure.
2. You might have to admit that a particular goal you'd written was not your own; it had been imposed on you by someone else.
3. You might be setting yourself up for embarrassment or ridicule; some of your goals, if they were seen by others, might be thought as frivolous.
4. You might be setting up the possibility of competition: if something you wanted was a collectible, there might not be that many of them around.
5. You might be setting up the possibilities for the consequences of success: people might no longer be willing to take care of you, make allowances for you or feel sorry for you; or people might start to expect even more from you, maybe even take advantage of you as you develop a reputation for achieving your goals.

These five reasons for your unwillingness to set goals are all possible unpleasant consequences. And, since you suspect that, if you did set goals, one or more of these consequences would likely happen, you don't set goals. What could be more sensible? You know that, despite what so many of the experts-in-living say about the importance of goal-setting, your having explicit goals will very quickly make you more unhappy, more frustrated, than you are now.

On the other hand, management consultants, guidance counselors and other experts have told us that the first solution to the many problems we face either as individuals, as groups, or even as an entire nation, involves our setting goals and dedicating our lives to meaningful purposes. We have been told that if we are confused, anxious, or depressed, it is because either our lives have no such worthwhile purpose, or that we have committed ourselves to trivial goals. It may be no accident that the most popular game for adults and children alike in the 1980's was *Trivial Pursuit*. According to the experts, the way to escape our petty existences is to set objectives and to clarify exactly what we want to achieve. In so doing, they say, we will escape our misery and depression and our feelings of irresponsibility, lack of commitment, selfishness, and indecision, and perhaps also remove the risk of that worst of all stigmata — mental illness. They ask us, for example, when we complain about our situation, just what exactly our goals are, what we'd like to be doing in five years, and so on.

As is now probably clear, we feel this approach is misguided. Many goals are no more than statements of what you think ought to be. As statements of what you actually want, they can be illusory. As paradoxical as it sounds, what you want is not necessarily what you say you want. This is why so many people are accused of not "knowing what they want." What you want is what you choose at any point in time without either necessarily knowing why, or having decided it in advance. On the other hand, what you say you want — your goals, objectives, hopes, dreams — may just be more rules you've added to all the others you are already carrying around with you. Goals are often yet another form of justification you give for your actions when asked why you did something: "I enrolled in Economics 401 because, if I want to make over $30,000 a year, I should get more training." And there it is again: the universal state-ment of should or ought, this time masquerading as a personal goal.

Goals and objectives may not be what you want at all; they are just as likely to be what you have been taught that you ought to want. Goal-setting is frequently rule-setting, and rules, even when you call them goals, often clash with what you will, in particular situations, choose to do.

There is one final reason to treat goals and objectives carefully. Goals are often seen as "ends," with the projects, programs, and recipes designed to achieve them seen as "means." Seeing things in terms of means and ends inevitably sets up the age-old means-ends distinction with its related, ever-debated question, "Do the ends justify the means?"

This distinction is phony. One cannot meaningfully categorize actions and other events into means and ends. As soon as some end is attained, it immediately becomes, at least potentially, a means to some new end, which will, when attained, itself become a possible new means, and on and on. Such temporary categorizing serves no useful purpose; it only confuses us and, worse, it focuses our attention on a fictitious future.

This logic of goals has frequently led individuals and nations to justify terrible actions because "they work." A lot of programs have "worked," but one must never lose sight of the price that is paid when actions are justified in terms of their presumed ends. The gas chambers and furnaces at Auschwitz also "worked." The anthropo-logist Margaret Mead was talking along the same lines when she said in 1942, "By working toward defined ends we commit ourselves to the manipulation of persons, and therefore to the negation of democracy."

Much more important to our dignity and the meaning of our lives is how things are accomplished. It is the attention to the proc-ess, rather than to the product, of our actions that will best safe-guard us from violations of humanity.

The earliest lawmakers of Western civilization realized this, and that is why Anglo-Saxon jurisprudence has emphasized "due process" as the cornerstone of our freedom.

The emphasis on how things are done, rather than what might eventually be achieved has been seen, over the seven hundred years since Magna Carta, to be the surest guarantee of the humane treatment of people – certainly in the field of criminal justice, where acts are frequently violent and the desire for revenge, reparation, and retribution overwhelming.

Summary

Setting goals, despite what the experts-in-living have written, is often a sure-fire way to add stress and discontent to your life. Goals may not be what you really want because they are frequently statements of what you have been taught to think you ought to want. That is, they are the universal statements of should or ought which, because of their incredible potential for hamstringing your intuitive dealing with your world, must be at least examined if not modified, made "hazier," and possibly even discarded in your search for serenity. To the extent that you are going to be able to deal intuitively with problems, whatever goals you set become irrelevant if not excess baggage to encumber you.

What you really want is what you really do. Wanting is best not spoken of as a verbal act – but as a non-verbal one. Never accept at face value what people tell you they want. What any person wants is what that person (non-verbally) chooses to do.

CHAPTER EIGHT

Filtering the World: Plans

Yvonne: *"Will I see you tonight?"*
Rick: *"I never make plans that far ahead."*

Humphrey Bogart in *Casablanca*

"A lot of people, especially this one psycho-analyst guy they have here, keeps asking me if I'm going to apply myself when I go back to school next September. It's such a stupid question, in my opinion. I mean, how do you know what you're going to do till you do it? The answer is, you don't. I don't think I am, but how do I know? I swear it's a stupid question."

J. D. Salinger, *Catcher in the Rye*

Planning is one of the most approved and recommended activities of all Americans, whether in our personal or professional lives. Some management consultants would have you believe that virtually nothing should be attempted without careful and systematic planning. It is universally portrayed as the touchstone of success.

Of all cultures, mainstream America loves to plan. Could it be that football has become our mania not only because of its violence and glamour, but also because it is a game in which formal planning actually takes up as much time as the execution of the plan?

Perhaps the same is true of one of our favorite card games — bridge (not the violence, the planning!). However, in a gentle chiding of the American yen for planning, Paul Hogan, the Australian

TV and movie personality, has said on CBS Television's 60 Minutes, "Life is not a dress rehearsal; don't plan it too much."

The best-known kind of planning these days is time management, a collection of techniques including prioritizing, scheduling, delegating, and otherwise organizing one's work. Diaries and date-books are available from a variety of companies all claiming to make these planning tasks easier to perform. The number of seminars in time management held by self-styled experts seems sometimes to approach the number of regularly scheduled college courses everywhere! Many people who attend these seminars and who purchase these date-books are probably helped to some degree by them, though at bottom the seminars appear to be little more than common sense, and the date-books only elegantly laid-out lists of "things to do" each day.

A date-book or calendar does not create a future of any kind; it is only a plan for what you'll do if—if you're still around, and if circumstances haven't changed beyond your expectations at the time you made the schedule entry. It is the kind of "what if" we will warn you about in Chapter 11, The Demise of Intuitive Action.

Planning is your attempt to provide guidelines for your actions in the future. It is the attempt to treat the world as closed rather than open; to create formulas that will relieve you of the freedom to choose later in exchange for the spurious security of certainty now; to develop techniques that can be relied on to provide effortless and ready-made answers to future problems, to eliminate the possibility of surprise. But it is even more than that: planning is actually an attempt to control the future itself, to pretend that it can be made less plastic, more predictable. We do it both as individuals and in groups, large and small. In this chapter we will talk about the pitfalls of planning as individuals. In the next chapter we'll apply these same ideas to planning in the business world.

There are those who, in examining their accomplishments over the years, see these as achievements planned for and worked toward over long periods of time. The successful businesses, the dividend income, the influential friends, the summer home in Maine, the jewels, furs, and fine cars, the memberships in exclusive clubs, all are regarded proudly as end-products of sustained and disciplined effort.

Unfortunately for our personal pride, such is not the case, no matter how much hindsight makes it seem so. We have been taught to talk of our successes as the results of our planning, but it only seems in retrospect that our plans contributed to these successes. At no time during the many years during which a person was working could he or she have described in any detail what now exists. Hindsight suggests that the person was "working towards" the happy state of affairs which now exists, that the current circumstances are "the fruit of his or her labors," but that is not what has actually happened at all. That person was just dealing at each point in time in the best way he or she could with situations as they were presenting themselves. The person may have "known what he or she wanted," but, we must ask, how does that imagined situation compare in detail with the happy events actually existing now? And, furthermore, if things had not turned out well, would that person still say that the current state of affairs had been planned for? Of course not! As the German philosopher, Nietzsche, put it, "Success has always been a great liar."

For every person who insists that he or she is where he is as a result of systematic and careful planning, there are many more who will insist with equal vigor that most aspects of life – certainly the important ones – seem to resist all attempts at such planning.

Before you throw your hands up in disgust and say, "But how can you live without planning for the future; how can you not plan for retirement, for example?", consider just what you do when "planning for retirement." You put money in the bank or other investments, period. You may say, "I have invested in this particular fund so that I'll be comfortable in my old age." But how that money will actually be used in the future cannot be stated with any certainty at the moment it is invested. You simply do not know exactly how you'll use the money, or even if you yourself will be around to use it at all.

How you plan for retirement – in which investments you put your money – is based on nothing more than what appears to be a good idea at this time, based on the information available to you now. The decision has nothing to do with the future, in the sense that it cannot now be affected by the future. How can it be? The future has not happened yet; it cannot affect anything we do now except, if you insist, by way of what we conventionally call our "expectations" or "projections."

What are "expectations" or "projections?" The Hopis have given us the best clue: the mental and the future are equivalent realities. Our expectations and plans are nothing more than our talk about the future, fueled by our wishes and hopes to control it. So, instead of asking what you expect to be doing five years from now, we suggest you ask how your expectations of five years ago match what you have to deal with now. When you do this, you will realize how futile and unnecessary your expectations really are.

There are two ways of seeing non-compulsory long-term investments for retirement, such as IRA's. First, the way these plans are usually sold is to ask the potential buyer to look ahead and say how much money he or she would like to have at some future time. Then the salesperson determines the size of the monthly payments by a formula. If things work according to the plan; that is, if the buyer lives, and if the company's own investment policies are sound – in other words, to the extent that the future contains no unpleasant surprises for the company – the desired amount of money becomes available at the end of the plan's term.

The second way, what we will call the intuitive way, reverses this approach and first looks at how much money one feels comfortable putting aside now. What such monthly outlays may amount to, all being well, in say twenty years, is of small import. The intuitive person is not concerned with what might happen in twenty years, or with what his or her financial needs are likely to be. He or she is living now, and if putting some amount aside now for whatever purpose, and at whatever time in the future, is felt to be important, it is done. But the intuitive person is not traumatized by threats of, or the need for, protection in an uncertain future. He or she sees all talk of the future as daydreaming; the future will be dealt with when it happens with whatever financial resources are at one's disposal at that time.

Another way that many people plan for their financial future is by taking out life insurance. Life insurance, according to its salespersons in their more candid moments, is fundamentally a bet between the insurance company and the insured that the latter will die, leaving the proceeds of the insurance contract to the beneficiaries, before an amount of money equal to those benefits (interest considerations ignored) has been paid to the company. People in huge numbers, particularly in the United States, are willing to take this bet. That is, when it comes to important things like money and the welfare of loved ones, people are not willing to bet on a long life for themselves; instead they bet on having a limited future. Indeed you may argue that it is not the future of the insured that is being planned for at all, but the future of the beneficiary.

This does not change anything that we have said. An attempt is still being made by someone, this time on behalf of someone else, to control the future, to make the future more benign than it might otherwise be. But is there not a more effective way of equipping your beneficiary for a fickle if not fictitious future? Yes, there is. It consists of doing what you can to enable that person to deal with the world as it may then present itself. In the sense of the old Chinese proverb, "Give a man a fish, and he eats for one day. Teach him to fish, and he eats for a lifetime," you should teach your beneficiary to fish, rather than just giving him or her a lot of fish.

What would it be like to live your life as though it will end soon, to indeed live it one day at a time? We think it would be, to say the least, filled with relationships which are much more charming, gracious, civil, and harmonious than those most people "enjoy" now. The relationships many have now are more likely to be endured than enjoyed.

Relationships within families, for example, are frequently bitter, jealous, and filled with acrimony and vicious backbiting — making one wonder whether there really ever was such a thing as "one big, happy family." Many people act as though they feel that they have all the time in the world in which to remediate real or imagined slights and hurts. They permit family feuds to go on for literally years. And, finally, they die with a lot of "unfinished business" to haunt those left behind.

Ask yourself, what could you do today to make someone in your family feel better about him or herself? How much more content would you feel immediately if you did just that? And, lastly, just what is stopping you from picking up the phone and getting a process of reconciliation started with someone you have been "on the outs" with? Would such a phone call hurt any more than the continued alienation you have felt for so long? Well, what are you waiting for?

There is another pleasant aspect to living one's life entirely in the present: it is the first step to helping you know what you want, this time without enlisting the aid of anyone else. During a recent conversation with a young woman presently contemplating what to do following college graduation, little more than a year away, she noted that she had been preparing for law school, but now was considering a stint in the Peace Corps. However, she said that neither really appealed to her. Most important to our discussion here is that if she were really interested in either choice, she would be doing something about it right now in the form of writing letters, taking aptitude tests and visiting law schools. She is not doing any of these things. This failure to act is not telling her what she truly wants to do. It is telling her, though, what she does not want to do, and such information is certainly not without value.

Another part of the conversation with this young woman involved her preferences for the approaching summer: "Do you know what I'd really like to do? Go to D.C. and spend two months with Mike. But I can't. I've got to stay and work. I'll have bills to pay in September."

There, you say, is that not an example of the future exerting its influence on the present? No, it is not. Consider, what is it exactly prompting the statement, "I'll have bills to pay in September."? It is things in the current situation: a bill in hand and the "memory" of what financial obligations existed last September. A new student, one who did not have to pay tuition and other college-related bills last September, will not likely be burdened with such feelings. Indeed, he or she will likely seem irresponsible to parents and friends because he/she is not talking about having the money available then. No, it is not the future exerting its influence; it is the past and the present. Once again, the future has disappeared into oblivion, where it belongs.

People who spend much of their time planning, that is, thinking about what they may do in the future, are often the same people who always seem to need to do something else first whenever a task presents itself. If most of what you do is plan, most of what you will have whenever your life is over are unrealized plans, expectations, hopes, and dreams – not accomplishments.

There is one sort of activity taking place in the present which attempts to deal effectively with an unknown future. It assigns specific probabilities in the form of prices we expect to pay or receive at specific points on the calendar to the items in which we are interested. This entire activity is called "the futures market." For example, a farmer may apply for a loan to buy a new piece of equipment for his business and need collateral. Some of this can be part of the income the farmer expects to receive when the crop is harvested and sold. How much he can expect is based on a myriad of factors including how many acres are under cultivation by our farmer and the many other farmers raising the same crop, as well as the weather, current supplies on hand, expected imports of that crop, and the anticipated needs in the Soviet Union and elsewhere. Futures investing is not for the timid!

However, there are many brave people who do invest in (some would say, "play") the futures market. And, each time they do, their aggregate activities of bidding, asking, buying, and selling establish prices in the future for the various commodities. But, and here is the important point, all this activity is taking place today and in the admitted absence of knowledge of the future. That is why this trading is so complex and why, when money is riding on it, it is approached so carefully. If, then, you insist on thinking about and planning for the future, we suggest you do it with at least equivalent care.

Just as you cannot re-live the past, you cannot pre-live the future. To attempt to do so is to incapacitate your ability to act now, to be sensitive to what is going on now, which is of paramount importance in cultivating your intuitive effectiveness.

Another aspect of living your life in the present instead of in the future is that you will be careful about making promises. Promises are obligations, commitments to act in the future, and few of them, unless there are severe penalties involved, ever seem to be kept. Those promises that are kept are often done with resentment and with a corrosive effect on relationships. When you do keep a promise happily, what you are actually doing is acting in harmony with the conditions in the current circumstances, not with the verbal promise made some time in the past. Most people repay debts, promissory notes, and loans not so much because they promised to and they are now keeping their word, but because the conditions in the current situation are such that if they don't make regular payments on the mortgage, auto loan, or student loan, something unpleasant is liable to happen.

You can only act now, in the present. When Scarlett O'Hara said at the end of *Gone With The Wind*, "Tomorrow I'll think of some way.... After all, tomorrow is another day," perhaps she was demonstrating that she was not merely the thoughtless and selfish creature thought by many. Perhaps she was wise enough to realize that we must wait until tomorrow arrives before we can act in it. Certainly, she was wise enough not to waste today worrying about tomorrow, and that is, it seems, wiser than most.

Summary

Planning involves the assumption that things will remain much the same as they are, that you can predict enough of the conditions that will be operating in the future so that your preparations and plans will proceed on course uninterrupted by unpleasant surprises.

Planning is an attempt to control the future before it happens as opposed to waiting to see what happens, and having the confidence to deal with it intuitively. Actions can only occur in the present, and the best guidelines for behavior are those present now and those that occurred in the past.

You add stress to your life to the extent that you try to set things up in advance – and then you are stuck with them. Deal with the present now, and with the future when, and if, it happens.

CHAPTER NINE

Filtering the World: Work

"The best laid schemes o'mice and men
gang aft agley."

Robert Burns

I n this short chapter, we will examine some of the practical im-
plications of the last two chapters for coping with your world of
work, particularly if you are a manager in that world.

As difficult as planning can be when tried by individuals, its
hazards increase exponentially when indulged in by groups. Dealing with one's own wants and needs, and how to obtain them, is
one thing. But it is a very different thing when one has to deal with
the wants, needs – and opinions on how to obtain them – of several
other people as well.

We said in the last chapter that Americans love to plan, and it
is when they are in groups that they love to plan most. Little can
be left to chance, to spontaneity, to serendipity. One of the chief
differences between the American way of rearing children and that
of the English is manifested in the way Americans organize children's recreation. In England, for example, children learn to play
soccer or cricket with a tennis ball in the street. When they play
with a real ball on a field, it is not likely to be a well-marked pitch,
and no adult is likely to be present to "officiate." Even at school,

the most organized sports are still intramural: a cricket game between school teams is a celebrated event. On the other hand, in
the United States, while young people do play sandlot baseball,
other children scarcely out of diapers are organized into supervised
leagues, wear uniforms, have uniformed adults officiating at all
games, and participate in serious tournament play for champion-
ship awards. Again, little can be left to chance, to the children's
own enterprise.

In government bureaucracies, planning has high status. There
are Directors of Planning with their own budgets, and paid attendance at planning seminars is considered an executive perk of the
highest order. Plans are typed up and bound in impressive volumes.
Not infrequently, an excellent new idea, brought in by a new addition to the agency's staff, will be turned down because it is "not in
the plan."

In this chapter, we act the part of the little boy who cried, "But
the Emperor isn't wearing any clothes!" We assert that planning, at
least as it is currently carried on, is wasteful of time, ineffective in
obtaining the desired results, and preemptive of more productive
activity. Later we will ask not, "If you don't know where you're going, how will you know if and when you've arrived?", as so many
management consultants do. We will ask instead, "If you don't know
where you are now, how will you be able to go anywhere at all?"

Formal planning in organizations, as with individuals in their
personal lives, is an excuse for procrastinating. Perhaps that is why
bureaucrats do so much of it, why they pay so much homage to it.
The PERT charts and the GANTT charts in the boardrooms of so
many of the corporations that use them are largely wasted exercises. These contrivances are abandoned just as soon as the situation changes from what we thought it would be – and change it
will! What we need most is nothing more than simple lists of things
to do today.

Coping effectively with the responsibilities of leadership in
agencies and corporations involves what William Lareau, in his
Conduct Expected, called the management of messes. This is to say
that, regardless of outward appearances and what management
would like you to believe, organizations are not organized. They

conduct their affairs largely by the "seat of the pants" in top management through policies and procedures which are followed only when it suits top management's purposes. As we will show, this is not necessarily bad. Indeed, we do recommend that system-atic organizational planning be de-emphasized, when it cannot be eliminated altogether particularly in new or rapidly expanding or-ganizations, or those operating in a fast-changing environment. What we are saying is that an organization is better run by intui-tive rather than analytic managers, with policies that take account of extenuating circumstances to permit managers flexible imple-mentation. Even in such a simple matter as setting an agenda for a meeting we see that, regardless of the order of business, what hap-pens to be important to the participants at the time the meeting is convened will determine what is talked about and when, in-cluding, if necessary, the scrapping of the entire agenda.

With the same inevitability of change we discussed in the last chapter, plans will inevitably break down. You do not think, for example, that the D-Day Invasion, an operation planned for over two years and involving hundreds of thousands of people, went off without a hitch, do you? No one who participated thinks so. When enterprises, large or small, have been carried through to suc-cess, we suggest that (a) what constituted "success" was continually redefined throughout; and (b) whatever plan was drawn up at the beginning had to be subjected to ongoing revision by individuals who, when things started to go "wrong," would step in, take charge, and improvise effectively to salvage the effort. When an engine on a DC-10 commercial aircraft blew up during flight in July 1989, what prevented the loss of life of everyone on board was not the crew's careful following of emergency rules, plans, and procedures. It was the intuitive expertise of the pilot gained over many years of flying under all kinds of contingencies.

We Americans have even institutionalized the failure of our planning efforts in every field from high technology to the kitchen in Murphy's Law, now well established as part of our national humor. What is Murphy's Law, if not a statement that plans will fail? (The kitchen version states that bread always falls jelly-side down, and that it is impossible to plan in advance which side to put the jelly on.) The elder General von Moltke said, "Plans do not survive the battle's opening shots," but perhaps heavyweight champ Mike Tyson said it best: "They all come in with plans, but they forget 'em quick."

Plans always need improvising. Indeed, it was the incapacity of the American military force for such improvisation that dealt the final death blow to the mission to rescue the hostages from Tehran. Our force's inability to "implement Plan B" or better, just "wing it," was imposed by the constraints of interservice rivalry. It was the overweening desire to simplify decisions regarding the reliability of applicants wanting to work for U.S. intelligence agencies that caused a catastrophic unquestioning reliance by the CIA on electronic lie-detector techniques throughout the 1980s. As one official, quoted in the *Wall Street Journal* (November 27, 1987), stated, "We have abandoned our competence in favor of the box. It absolves you from having to think about the problem, and it's a great way to protect yourself."

On a more historical note, the brilliant victory of the English fleet under Nelson over the combined French and Spanish fleets at Trafalgar in 1805 was due to their new system of flag signals which enabled them to adapt to circumstances as they developed. The French and Spaniards, on the other hand, had to rely on plans which had been drawn up and agreed upon before the battle.

It has been suggested by some Monday morning stock market quarterbacks that the stock market crash of October 19, 1987, was considerably worsened by computers which had been earlier programmed to sell at some future signal — thus absolving brokers and investment account managers of the need to decide on that October 19th what to do when that signal actually occurred.

The habit of inventorying the present can also be performed by groups of people. Indeed, management seminars and retreats must be the group equivalent of an individual's inventorying of the present, if they are to have lasting value. However, if you are a manager, you have certainly noticed that most corporate training or planning seminars emphasize future-oriented, rational, analytic, systematic, data-oriented approaches. They encourage their participants to prepare ordered lists of priorities, to specify goals, and to make checklists. We encourage you to do exactly the opposite. Do not list priorities. Do not specify goals. Instead, perform an intensive inventory of the present, all the while recognizing that such an inventory is not a checklist of things to do. It is a detailed description of things as they are now. You will very quickly discover that such an inventory is infinitely more valuable to you than lists of priorities, goals, and objectives.

An inventory is the vehicle by which things get done, not the lame and tame documents which emerge from your own or your organization's present planning efforts, only to get shelved and forgotten.

It is only the sticklers for proper form and procedure who complain when managers are intuitive and sensitive to contingencies, when they go with their guts regarding personnel placement, or anything else. And the intuitive managers are invariably right when they ignore the verbal obstacles comprising the company procedures manuals. In his book, *Demanaging America*, Richard Cornuelle encourages managers to let people do their jobs, to free workers from front-office control. He asks us to recognize that the true expert in any job is most likely not the consultant brought in from out of town, but the person who actually does that job. This is because that person is the closest to, the most intimate with, the most sensitive to, the job's conditions and demands.

De-managing is not delegating, and it is a lot more than just managing by objectives. It involves the recognition of where the expertise lies and liberating its skills. An executive who de-manages never tells his or her subordinates how to do their jobs. He or she assured that they knew how before they were hired. Telling people how to do their jobs constitutes an intrusion between the job's conditions and demands and the worker. The executive simply tells people what he wants, and when.

The still-dominant theory of personnel management in both corporations and bureaucracies is called "Scientific Management." Developed by Frederick Winslow Taylor in the late Nineteenth Century, it embodies the view that organizations are composed of "slots," each slot having a "job description" into which a person is fitted. You may wonder whether Taylor, who died in 1915, got this idea from the then recently-developed, industry-wide use of interchangeable machinery parts. We do not know. What we do know, though, is that people, even those with the same job descriptions, are not and never have been, interchangeable.

While individuality was certainly ignored in earlier days, companies will be dangerously threatened if they ignore it in the computerized global economy of the nineties where commercial success will be based more on a company's ability for creativity, coordination on a broad scale, flexibility, and product/service modification at short notice than on the year-after-year assembly-line production of unvarying products. The techniques which served Henry Ford well are not likely to work for a corporation which coordinates the manufacture of semi-conductors in Taiwan with their assembly in Singapore or Mexico for marketing in the U.S. and Europe.

Robert Reich says in his *Tales of a New America*, that in the new world economy entrepreneurial efforts must focus on many small ideas rather than (as in the days of Henry Ford) a few big ones. Hence management must not manage, it must not direct, set goals, or solve problems for workers. It must lead by creating a context within which employees can do these things for themselves – a context whose details will demand the most imaginative efforts of intuitive entrepreneurs.

What happens in organizations which are de-managed? First, the morale tends to be high. This is because, in freeing workers to decide for themselves how to do their jobs, they seek the best way they themselves can devise. Second, formal policies and procedures take a back seat to results. The best example of this sort of organization is the Israeli Air force, an organization in which everyone from the lowliest clerk to the highest-level executive is on a first-name basis. This organization's current score against its chief competitor, the Syrian Air Force, is 89-0.

In late 1987, newspapers reported an excellent example of the creative things that happen when managers expose themselves to the actual contingencies of situations in which their businesses operate. Bob Price, the operator of a shopping center maintenance business in Sydney, Australia, decided, after spending a hot day loading shopping carts onto a truck, that an easier way was needed. What emerged from his efforts was the Kelpie Kargo Truck which has a flatbed and tailgate that can be lowered to ground level. It remains to be seen whether the vehicle (conceived in Australia and assembled in Taiwan of 80% American parts) will sell well, but that is only part of the point being made here. If Mr. Price had stayed in his office that day while his employees worked outside, he would likely never have had the idea of a lowerable flatbed nor been willing to invest $5 million in its development.

Creativity and innovation are not usually found in complex, multi-hierarchied vertical organizations, but in "flatter," simply-organized companies where the decision-making power is not separated from the people with continuous opportunities for an intuitive dealing with the environment in which the company operates. Indeed, when the people on the front-line are ignored and seen as "grunts" who are insensitive to "higher-order" (usually short-term political) priorities, tragedies such as the Challenger space-shuttle follow.

What also happens in complex, highly structured organizations is that their managers, who themselves are perfectly comfortable with an intuitive approach to problems, have to deal with higher-ups, members of the Board, and stockholders who continue to demand data to support what they call executive decision-making. In these instances, data are often marshalled after the fact and perhaps even fabricated to substantiate what the manager wants to do. This, we fully believe, happens more often than not in both one's personal as well as business dealings.

Most of our greatest accomplishments as a civilization appear to have been made almost haphazardly. To what extent did Gottlieb Daimler "work towards" the automobile of the 1980s? To what extent did J. S. Bach "work towards" the music of Beethoven, Berlioz, or Bloch? And, to labor the point just a little, to what extent did Michael Faraday "work towards" the hydro-electric dam? The answer is obvious: not at all. It only appears so in retrospect,

as one sees history as though it were planned. Planning, particularly formal and inflexible planning, like rigid goal setting, is largely
futile. As Rod McKuen says, "Life is what happens while you're
planning it."

But perhaps all is not hopeless for the intuitive executive in an
organization which refuses to dispense with its armamentarium of
published policies and procedures, its planning divisions. In such
an organization, the illusion of planning's importance can be main-
tained by continuing its existence while staffing it with personnel
who are already demonstrably useless to the organization but who,
given the rules of the personnel system (themselves among the
chief obstacles to intuitive management) governing hiring, firing,
and so forth, cannot be fired. (We are told that even Chairman
Gorbachev has had considerable difficulty getting rid of his dead
wood, and it still remains open to question whether he or they will
prevail!) There, in the Planning Division, these people can feel
very important without doing any harm beyond wasting reams of
paper with their Five-Year Plans. In this way, the Planning Division becomes rather like The Leper Colony in the film, *Twelve
O'Clock High* (one of the finest management training films ever
made). The Leper Colony was the B-17 bomber designated by the
Group Commander to which a navigator was assigned "if he
couldn't find the men's room," or where a bombardier was assigned
"if he couldn't hit his plate with his spoon." The Group Commander's logic was that the resulting embarrassment and interde-
pendence would force anyone assigned to this particular airplane
to perform so well that he would soon be reassigned.

Our suggestion that bureaucracies set up an office of planning
is not quite the same. There are people working in bureaucracies
who will never perform at anything above marginal levels. Since
something must be done with them (as we said, they cannot be
fired), what better place than in a planning section which by its
very nature is usually useless?

Is there an alternative to abandoning the present in favor of
analyzing the past, or planning for a fictitious future, either as individuals or as corporate entities? There is. It is the intuitive approach against which planning is merely a pale substitute.

Summary

Much money and other resources are spent by companies and public agencies in planning. Most of these resources are wasted, and yet many competent managers and executives are tremendously successful without any formal planning. They deal with events as they happen, based on the totality of their past experiences, whether or not they can tell you why they are doing what they are doing. Such executives accept as given that the world is fluid, unpredictable, and infinitely changeable. Aside from labor and persistence, successful people do not know exactly how they became successful, and they do not pretend to. They have just done all along what seemed like a good idea at the time.

It is undoubtedly difficult not to think about, prepare for, plan for, the future — whether as individuals or as groups. Indeed, entire schools of thought in mathematics and logic have been formed based chiefly on whether any possible decision could be decided in advance. Needless to say, we believe that decidability in advance is a vain hope. Many of the problems of your life lie in the difficulty you have in not thinking about the future; in your thinking in terms of should and ought; not in your inability to solve all problems in advance. Stated another way, the problem is not that you cannot set up a system which will make decisions automatically for you later when needed, but that you want to set up such a system!

CHAPTER TEN

Obstacles to
Intuitive Action

*"Man is not troubled by events, but by
the meaning he gives to them."*

Epictetus

*"It's not what folks know that's the problem;
it's what they know that ain't so."*

Josh Billings

We have been saying that the really important choices in your life or your business should never be made rationally and logically. We don't mean that such choices should be made in the heat of anger or sexual passion, either. The danger of acting during intense emotion is that your current feelings distort the influence of all other contingencies operating at the time. When your anger, passion or grief subsides, those other aspects begin to make themselves felt again and, if you have acted in haste, you then find yourself free to repent at leisure.

Neither do we mean to say that the event instigating the anger or other emotion is not important. We mean for you to allow events to take their place with all the events in your past to give you an overall balanced basis for whatever action you take.

How long need you wait? Again, there are no rules. Let's say the more significant the event, the more intense the emotion, and the more drastic and irreversible the action comtemplated, the

101

longer you should wait. This is a given rule. We can tell it fits our definition because of the appearance of the word "should". Use it, if in retrospect, it works for you, if you feel comfortable with the results. If it does not work for you, if you do not feel comfortable with the consequences, drop it, and let your emotions have heavier sway. Eventually you may derive your own rule.

One of our society's most powerful obstacles to intuitive action is the pervasiveness of television. Television's most insidious influence on our culture as a whole is not that it has discouraged us from reading; not that it has enabled us to deal only superficially with issues; not even that it has exposed us to all that is banal in entertainment or that it has made us want so many things we do not need; but that it has destroyed our ability to feel intensely for long enough to cultivate effective intuitive habits.

It has done this in at least two ways. First, although television will on occasion permit us to see the face of catastrophe, atrocity, and tragedy close up, the timing of the presentation is arranged so that commercial interruptions occur frequently enough so that we will not remain horrified for too long. Scenes of tragedy have less impact on us if those scenes are quickly followed by clean American children eating cereal, or nubile young women drinking fruit juice. Our anger, horror, and sadness at the brutality wanes just as quickly.

Television has encouraged a desultory, vicarious, and detached approach to the world also because of the technology of the instant replay, and more recently, the universal availability of video-cassette recorders. Why should we live each moment of our lives as intensely as we can, when one can see all that is really important on television over and over and over again? Just how many times did we see President Kennedy get shot, to be followed by just how many repeats of Jack Ruby killing Lee Harvey Oswald? How many times were we shown the Challenger space shuttle exploding?

It might be argued that instant replay actually augments the impact of the environment on us, increasing our ability to react appropriately; that TV screens and filters the world for us, sifting out the trivia. We do not agree. The frequently repeated airing of one event, no matter how important that event is judged to be (by media people), must of necessity push other events into the background so that the world, even the world of television, is itself distorted.

But, you may say, if I don't watch TV, I won't know what's going on. What if important "newsworthy" events happen; how will I know? We are not suggesting that you give up on TV altogether. Television is often a vehicle for full-length films and even stage-plays, whose value we'll note in a moment. There are also excellent documentaries but when really important events occur, you'll surely find out, if only by your acquaintances asking you if you've heard that... It is true, though, that there will be many things you won't hear about. You won't hear about the several serious traffic accidents that occur in your city every day to people whom you do not know nor are ever likely to meet. You won't see the latest episodes of the shallow soap operas and sit-coms that fill TV's so-called prime time and through which so many of us live our own lives vicariously. You won't hear about the homicides or the household fracases which feed TV's insatiable appetite for violence and tragedy. You won't puzzle over the meaning for your own wallet of announcements that a particular new government program "will cost taxpayers $11 billion over the next five years." Nor will you be up on the latest sales of water-beds or automobiles.

You will, therefore, want less of the gimmicks and gadgets endlessly thrust in front of you. But, even more important, you will not, if you watch less TV, feel stressed by and called upon to deal with, things that are in reality, far beyond your control: the sorry state of our nation's schools, the drug menace, the molestation of children in day-care centers, the abuse of the elderly in nursing homes, the homeless. You will not worry about what you should do about any of these things (assuming, of course, that there is more to them than mere media and interest-group hype) beyond what you can do yourself to care for yourself, your own loved ones, and your own immediate community. And for this, you do not need to watch television's superficial and distorted view of the helpless and profligate flailing of government bureaucrats.

Our intuitive abilities would be better served by spending more time at the live theater than in front of the TV. Failing that, full-length movies are a step in the right direction. At least they allow our emotions free exercise, uninterrupted by commercials for deodorant soap or toothpaste, particularly when the movie has special meaning for us because of the subject it is treating. What better material for the intuitive activity of the young black girl than *The Color Purple*, of the young Jewish girl than *Yentl*, of the jaded entrepreneur than *Save the Tiger*, of the career woman questioning her choice twenty years earlier than *The Turning Point*, of the small-town teen-ager than *The Last Picture Show*, or of the recently-divorced woman striving to keep her new-found identity than *An Unmarried Woman*? And what could be a better example of the transformation from a rule-regulated harridan to an intuitive and, thereby, freer, more pleasant, and so much happier soul than before, than Katharine Hepburn in *The African Queen*?

The live theater, by contrast, is exactly that: LIVE! The emotions evoked in the audience by Shakespeare, O'Neill, Tennessee Williams, or Arthur Miller, particularly if the acting is of high caliber, are as close to the real thing as one can get, and our intuitive capacities, especially regarding human relationships, are broadened tremendously.

The intense feelings generated by direct contact with people and events can be quite frightening. This is the secret of TV's popularity: it rarely upsets us, and then only when necessary to sell us on something. Intense feelings can get you into real trouble. They can get you accused of "acting out," of being "out of control," "childish," or "irrational." This fearsome characteristic of feelings causes nurses on psychiatric wards to plead with psychiatrists to tranquilize patients whose anger might be quite understandable and easily dealt with if only they were listened to; and it has made heroes of those movie stars who appear able to control their feelings, to have walled off their emotions, or to have no feelings at all: Sylvester Stallone as Rambo, the characters played by John Wayne and Clint Eastwood, and Leonard Nimoy's Mr. Spock. Andy Warhol expressed the feelings of many Americans when he said, "I want to be a machine."

Despite this societal proscription of displays of feeling, however, people *do* feel. They seem actually to *need* to feel, and much that is wrong in our society may be due to the search for "kicks" in a world which has dulled so many almost into insensibility. The drug pandemic, the raucous rock music, the sexual promiscuity, even the plethora of horror movies and books all can be seen as extreme ways of getting you to *feel*. One wonders which one is more disturbed: the psychiatric inpatient, sexually abused for years as a child, whose feelings of rage and despair have been so ignored and even ridiculed that she smashes a window and uses the shards to cut her arms repeatedly as if to prove to herself that she is still alive and still capable of feeling; or the supposed normal person who pays to have his name superimposed on the soundtrack of a football game so that he can hear through the crowd's roar his name instead of that of Staubach, Dorsett, or Sayers.

The answer to the alienation and depression, however, is not in drugs or even electronic fakery in one form or another. It is putting an end to living vicariously. It is coming once again into direct contact with real people, real things, and the world's own uncontrived contingencies.

The most potent set of obstacles to intuitive dealings with our world is our own thinking and talking about it. One can be thinking many things while trying to respond effectively, in social situations in particular. Is my tie straight? Is my fly zipped? Did that shaving cut heal cleanly? Is my slip showing? Does the color of my blouse clash with my jacket? Am I being too assertive? Not assertive enough? Did I just say the wrong thing? All of these thoughts constitute obstacles to intuitive action. They all render you less sensitive to the situation's contingencies. While paying attention to your own actions, you let significant aspects of other people's behavior slip by you.

You, actually talking, do all this and more in the way of creating obstacles to contingency-shaped action. This is because, in addition to diverting your attention to yourself and away from the social situation you're in, your talking will suppress what would otherwise be happening. Of course, some talking on your part cannot be avoided, but it must be kept to a minimum if you are going to sense what is going on with the other participants in the discussion.

But there is yet another reason why your talking too much will create obstacles to intuitive action for you. Your words constitute your analysis of what is going on, both in the subject matter under discussion, and in the social dynamics of the argument itself. The former, certainly, is what the various members of your group want to hear, and they will be uncomfortable with you if you seem reluctant to speak your mind. They may even accuse you of not contributing to the discussion. But regardless of which of these two aspects you talk about, the more you talk, the more you will tend to convince yourself, as you are attempting to convince the others, that you are right, and that your analysis is an accurate portrayal of what is going on. That is, you will convince yourself that you understand what is happening and, when the discussion is over and you return to a presumably direct involvement with the issue at hand, you'll tend to respond more to your analysis of that aspect of the world rather than to the world itself. As Sam Rayburn, long-time Speaker of the U.S. House of Representatives, once said, "You ain't learning anything when you're talking."

A few years ago one of the authors had the responsibility of supervising young Ph.D.'s in their clinical work with severely disturbed patients. Much of the treatment took place in group therapy where the language of the patients was the focus of our efforts. Following the first of these sessions with a new clinician, he was asked what he thought of a certain patient. He launched into a lengthy statement of the patient's difficulties, including diagnosis, probable etiology of the case, possible predisposing family dynamics, prognosis, treatment recommendations, and discharge planning. Such a lengthy analysis made it possible for the author to point out to the new clinician that his analysis was much heftier than the data it was presumably based on, that he hadn't listened or observed that particular patient anywhere near enough to say anything more than, perhaps, "She is a very troubled young woman. Period." The danger, once again, was that the clinician's treatment of the patient would immediately begin to be based not on her behavior, but on his analysis. Now, given the requirements of insurance companies, with their rules, it is not possible to treat without diagnosis. But the intuitive clinician will speak very carefully about the case.

Here is an example of how the words of other people can get in the way between yourself and your world. Suppose, upon entering a friend's living room, you notice for the first time a rug of Southwestern design hanging on the wall. You say how much it appeals to you. Notice how your further responses to the rug will be different depending on what your friend now says:

(a) "Yes, that's a fine old rug of the Two Grey Hills pattern. It was made over a two-year period by a Navajo woman who sold it to me in Window Rock, Arizona."

(b) "Oh, that! It's just a piece of junk. They're mass-produced in Peru. The guy at the flea market in Detroit had fifty more just like it."

Now, even before you make another move toward the rug, to touch it or to examine it more closely, you are predisposed to see it differently. Furthermore, unless you have some familiarity with Indian rugs, you're likely to be fooled if your friend gave you the first answer, but the rug really was mass-produced in South America. How much more sensitive to the rug's actual history would you be if your friend had told you nothing at all?

It is not easy for any of us to be silent. We are trained from a very early age to demonstrate what we know by explaining it, or to indicate what we want by just saying it. That is part of the Greek rational tradition we have spoken of a while back. But our explanations of what we know are so often illusory. Indeed, as we saw in the statement by Asvaghosa in Chapter 2, anything we say in a situation is bound to be inadequate. Language is linear (earlier we said that words come tumbling out of our mouths in "chains") but the workings of nature are holistic, non-linear, and infinitely interdependent. We all know many things we cannot discuss coherently, but that does not mean we cannot deal effectively with them.

Another unfortunate consequence of analyzing situations too quickly and then acting on the basis of our labels is the self-fulfilling prophecy. In these cases we act toward people on the basis of our worst fears rather than if we gave them the benefit of the doubt. We see this not only in the clinical treatment of patients, but also in schools. Teachers are influenced by derogatory remarks made about their students by the latters' teachers in earlier grades — even when there has been little basis for such remarks. The intuitive schoolteacher, like the intuitive clinician, will remove this obstacle to his or her contingency-shaped actions towards the children by paying guarded attention to reports by educational diagnosticians as well as other teachers.

Even the slightest tendency on your part to label your own responses prompts you to act differently than you would if you did not label them. If you just allow your past to guide you, you'll be the most effective you can be. But if you say to yourself something like, "I don't think this is going to work out," then you'll act hesitantly — whether or not you realize it — and, with its incredible ability to be sensitive to even the most subtle aspects of your actions, both your physical and social environments will respond accordingly. They will see that you're unsure, that you feel the situation won't work out, and, lo and behold, it doesn't!

We have noticed, to our dismay, that when skiing cross-country down a steep and narrow trail, it is only when we say to ourselves, "This trail is too tough for me — I'm going to fall," that we do indeed fall. We have noticed a perceptible increase in our skiing skills when we force ourselves not to think about how difficult the trail is or whether we've ever handled one this tough before.

How is this done? The best way is to pay attention only to the details of the situation: the whiteness of the snow, the freshness of the breeze, the sound made by your skiis, perhaps even the beauty of it all. But not to your labels! Let that wait until you're at the bottom of the trail!

When you think about your own reactions to a situation instead of not-thinking about them, it is almost impossible to keep notions of "should" or "ought to" out. Saying, "This hill is too tough," or "This carburetor is too complicated," are just another way of saying, "I shouldn't be able to do this." And the next thing you know, you can't do it, you've failed, and worst of all, you're "a failure." A particular instance of your saying something has turned into a label for your entire being! All because you thought about your own actions instead of just letting yourself go, and doing. Just do! You'll be very surprised at the outcome.

One of the most tragic examples of our own words crippling our ability to act intuitively is found in many cases of impotence. Here the individual says to himself, "Everything is perfect, the atmosphere is great, the music lovely, she so beautiful and willing, and I should be able to," or, perhaps, "but I shouldn't (for some reason or other) be enjoying this." And so he is ineffective. He has raised enough obstacles to his intuitive involvement so that, instead of being sensitive to the situation and its contingencies, he is bound up by his silent verbal reactions to it.

Analogy is another of the more tragic examples found in talking about a difficult situation. Americans have a tremendous propensity for construing situations as metaphor, rather than sticking close to the concrete data. Perhaps we believe, as Aristotle did, that the use of metaphor is "The Mark of Genius." In any case, an incredible number of articles in business journals and magazines have been dedicated to seeing the competitive business environment as "war," particularly of the World War II variety, and corporate boardrooms as battle staff headquarters. We also see our favorite sport, football, as war, again of the WWII kind. Perhaps, since that war was the last one that we won, we behave as the late psychologist Abraham Maslow suggested. We treat all conflicts, at least verbally, just like it. Actually, what Maslow said was, "When the only tool you have is a hammer, you tend to treat everything as a nail."

Interestingly enough, when we Americans were actually involved in a war, one quite unlike WWII, we reversed the analogy and saw the war as a business endeavor, with "body-count" as a sort of index of profitability.

Do we need to say that in both cases, tragedy occurs? We lose markets to foreign competition, and we lose wars to foreign armies.

A humorous example of how words get in between ourselves and our world is this dialogue attributed to Abraham Lincoln:

Lincoln: I would like to ask my opponent how many legs does he think a horse has?

Opponent: A horse has four legs, sir!

Lincoln: Now, sir, would you tell these fine people and me, if we were to call the tail a leg, how many legs would the horse have?

Opponent: Well, Mr. Lincoln, if we were to call the tail a leg, then the horse would have five legs!

Lincoln: Wrong, sir! Because our calling the tail a leg will not *make it* a leg!

The use of analogy and metaphor in our attempts to deal effectively with our world leads to increases in stress, because we permit dubious and simplistic analyses clouding our view to intervene between us and our world. Analogies, as rules more given than derived, increase the distance between whatever more concrete terms we could use and the actual contingencies operating in the world. But in the corporate boardroom concrete thinking is derided as unimaginative in favor of the supposed more creative obscure and abstruse analyses of the management consultant or the computer modeler.

But even if one can stop talking, how can one stop thinking? Can you learn to voluntarily, at any time and at any place, stop thinking? One is reminded of the old party demonstration where one is asked to think of anything except apples. And, of course, you find that you absolutely can not get the idea of apples out of your head. The key is not to not-think of apples, but to not-think at all. But how?

One way is to engage in activity requiring little if any thought: house cleaning, lawn mowing, car washing, superhighway auto driving, or house painting. However, the most interesting things happen when you do this. Einstein once said that he had to be extremely careful while shaving since it was often just then that he would be seized by a very provocative thought, spontaneously as if from nowhere, causing him to jump. But as we saw in Chapter 2, thoughts do not come from nowhere. They come from the world's contingencies acting on us, and Einstein's thoughts were so elegant and innovative because he was, because of a past we can only guess at, incredibly more sensitive to them than the rest of us. And perhaps it was Isaac Newton's recognition that his own analyses would interfere with his intuitive processes of discovery which led him to say, "Hypotheses non fingo" (I feign no hypotheses).

If you cannot stop thinking, perform an inventory: repeat exactly what happened, what was said by all participants, including yourself, in the situation with which you are trying to deal. Remember particularly the feelings expressed, the facial gestures, the body movements, as well as precisely what was said. Relax and crawl inside the skin of each person involved.

Everything you need to act effectively in the situation is already available to you. Otherwise, how could you visualize in any detail what you think you want? All you have to do is access it. Ernest Holmes, developer of the Science of Mind – and the Church of Religious Science based on it – said, "Nothing more will ever be provided for our good than has already been provided for us." Intuitive choice is not seeing the future; it is feeling the past and the present.

You can also create options. As time progresses, you will intuitively select the option most appropriate. Indeed, in setting up the options, you'll feel which ones can even be rejected up front. Some examples are writing a letter, perhap in anger (which you can decide later whether or not to mail); making restaurant, opera, travel, or car-repair reservations (which you then have the option of keeping or breaking as eventual circumstances dictate); laying money aside in a special account (which you can then either use for that special purpose, or just let it accumulate interest); or taking two meals out of the freezer to defrost (leaving the choice of which one to prepare until you get home).

Sleeping on a problem is another device many people use to allow time for the contingencies in the situation to resolve themselves. Sometimes, when you wake, you seem to know what to do without anything in the situation being any clearer. Other times, if the contingencies have taken the form of dreams, what you want and do not want will become clear as you spend your first few waking minutes interpreting those dreams.

Lastly, there is a device suggested by an artist friend who, when he finds his sketches and drawings too pedestrian, takes a fresh board and, pencil or brush in hand, deliberately violates whatever rules he thinks are prompting his conventional work. The results, he says, are often startling.

In all of these examples you are not-choosing. You are deliberately deferring a choice until later while allowing the contingencies in the situation to unfold and further make themselves felt on you.

As a last resort, if you absolutely must have some verbal guidance to get you started, let it be indirect and non-specific — such as is provided by the I Ching. This is an augury which works by leading you through a set of procedures designed to arrive at one of sixty-four statements any one of which (rather like your newspaper's daily horoscope) actually could be helpful in handling your current quandary.

Finally, when you do act, watch what you do with confidence and enthusiasm. Watch for that moment when you smile spontaneously. Then you'll know you've made the right move!

Summary

The chief obstacles to intuitive action are your own talking and thinking — your analysis and understanding of the situation you are attempting to deal with — the problem you are trying to solve.

This talking and thinking often take the form of given rules — universal statements of should and ought, although more situation-specific derived rules may also get in the way, as well as the plans that you feel need to be adhered to.

Your analysis of a situation should be resisted until it absolutely forces itself on you — till it can no longer be disregarded by you.

CHAPTER ELEVEN

The Demise of Intuitive Action

"The more we live by our intellect,
the less we understand the meaning of life."

Leo Tolstoy

"Your intellect may be confused
but your emotions will never lie to you."

Roger Ebert

In the last chapter we examined some obstacles to intuitive action, some things which you need to overcome if you are to be truly sensitive to the contingencies of any situation. We discussed the distorting effect intense emotions can have on intuitive action, and we noted the unfortunate effect that television has had on the expressing of feelings and emotions. Most important, we discussed your own talking and thinking as obstacles to intuitive action, especially when they take the form of on-the-spot analyses of whether you can or should be able to deal effectively with a situation. Obstacles may take the form of labels – or, in the case of clinical professionals, diagnoses – and tell you how to deal with the situation.

Language has frequently been touted as the device by which we humans are able to deal with the world so much more effectively than other species. This may be true, but it should not blind you to words acting as a curtain which can cloud or obscure your vision, sensitivity and intuitive dealing with the world. It might even be said that intuitive action begins to decay and die the more verbal one becomes. We see this in children. As their language develops, they become less intuitive, less contingency-influenced, and more rule-regulated. Before a baby responds to words, it is completely intuitive. The very process of its rearing, however, is permeated with rules on what should be done and how to do it — regardless of how the child would behave if given the freedom to do it him/herself. The logic of the parent or teacher is that the child would not act in its own best interest if given that freedom. While this is certainly true some of the time, it is frequently the case — particularly as the child grows up — that he or she begins to know better than adults what is in her "best interest."

Unfortunately, from our point of view, by the time the young person's rearing and schooling is completed, words and rules and "rational thinking" have come to govern a large part of behavior, with intuitive propensities downplayed if not even ridiculed or punished. It is usually in mid-life that people begin to recognize the limitations imposed by rationality, and start to "go with their guts."

There are some words which are particularly implicated in the demise of intuitive action, and in this chapter we explain why, to be intuitive, you will purge your vocabulary of them.

First, the words can't and won't. The intuitive person translates these into simple declaratives. Instead of saying, "I can't play the piano," or, "I won't go anywhere with her!", the intuitive person simply says, "I do not play the piano," and "I choose not to go anywhere with her." Note that these statements are in the present tense: I do not and I choose not. "Won't" says that no circumstance could ever arise which might prompt you to do something you don't do now. It is a statement about your behavior in the future, and intuitive people don't make such statements. If the future is a fiction then the less said of it, the better. Hence the intuitive person uses the future tense of verbs very carefully. Instead of saying, "It will happen;" or "I will do that," he or she prefers, "It is happening;" or, "I am doing that."

It is from such a view of life that the intuitive person looks quizzically at such questions like this one often asked at personal planning and goal-setting seminars: "What is the single, most important thing you would leave undone if you were to die today?" As you saw in an earlier chapter, the intuitive person does live life as if death were imminent. There is, therefore, nothing left undone.

Following "can't" and "won't," the next words that young people are frequently encouraged to take seriously are, "What if…?" Intuitive people, refusing to worry about a fictitious future, do not indulge in what-ifs. They do not know what they will do if something or other happens. They just wait and see. Even if all the details of the what-if could be spelled out, the intuitive person knows that he or she still cannot predict what reactions will represent their best dealing with that situation.

This can be quite frustrating for such people as that new professional breed, the "futurists," or for the market researcher who wants to know whether a new product will sell. The personnel assessment specialist may want to know whether an applicant will do well in a particular position or training program. That is, "'What if we sell Brand X with a green and white label instead of a red and white label?" or "'What if we hire John into the project manager position?" Many surveys and other instruments have been designed over the years to answer such questions, and the results have been mixed, the most celebrated failure being the prediction that the Ford Edsel would sell well. But while corporations, in order to safeguard their stockholders' investments, must at least attempt such predictions of "what if," you, as an intuitive individual, do not need to. You can, most of the time, afford the luxury of just waiting to choose what to do when the circumstance arises.

Further child-rearing and schooling introduce words even more destructive to an intuitive dealing with events. "Revenge" and "vindication" are two such words and they are not found in the language of the intuitive person. These words are the extreme opposite of the forgiveness discussed in Chapter 4. Actions in the name of revenge or vindication are certainly far more prevalent in human behavior than are actions in the name of forgiveness. Alexander Theroux, writing in *Harpers* in October, 1982, suggested that, "along with love and war, with which themes, let us say, it has more than passing acquaintance, revenge is the single most informing element of world literature."

What are revenge and its brother, vindication? They are words describing how you feel when you are involved in redressing a grievance, righting the balance; when you feel victimized, taken advantage of, or injured. But is this redress an attempt to remove the hurt or pain in the process psychologists call negative reinforcement, such as your taking an aspirin to get rid of a headache? No, it isn't. Indeed, in his or her actions, the person seeking revenge seems almost to want to hold on to the hurt. It is as if, like Shakespeare's Iago (in *Othello*), the person hates first and then afterwards looks for an excuse to hate. The person seems to need the hurt to provide a justification for what he or she is set on doing anyway.

Revenge rarely seems to restore a balance, to return to the perpetrator what was "rightfully" his or hers. It is not as if you were short-changed, and now you want to adjust the balance. In getting even or settling an old score, one behaves instead as if the old given rule, "Don't get mad, get even," or "An eye for an eye," is prompting the action. And, as long as you follow such rules, as long as you encourage your children to follow such rules, the world as it is, with all its opportunities and pleasures, passes you by, because all your efforts and attention are focused on the "evildoer."

You should remember also that it is not so much what happens to the person upon whom revenge is being inflicted that is important, as to the perpetrator of that revenge. It is what you feel, or what you expect to feel, when you take revenge that is the driving force behind the action.

However, there is no relief, is there? There is more likely remorse and fear, if not guilt. And if your enemy is precisely the kind of intuitive person we have been describing throughout this book, think of how tormented you will be as he or she continually forgives you all your efforts at retaliation and injury.

Once you dedicate your life to vindication, the issue is not resolved until your life itself is over. Even if your "enemy" dies, the scales of justice still sway. As long as you live, the "bottom line" has yet to be written, and at any moment, the impartial universe can deal you a blow which you could well interpret as being in your now-dead enemy's behalf. The intuitive person knows that seeking revenge, or even just talking of it, is to involve yourself in a life-long moral quest of self-righteousness guided by your own given rules regarding how things ought to be, and how you are given license to set them straight. Consider Romans, 12-19: "...avenge not yourself, but rather give place unto wrath: for it is written, Vengeance is mine; I will repay, saith the Lord." Whether you are one of those who believe that the personal pronouns "I" and "mine" in the quotation refer to God, to the impartial universe (who will repay), or to some vestige of the repugnant act lying in the perpetrator which will fester inside and corrode him or her, the message in this case is clear: forgive and, if you can, forget.

Yet another word which is taught early to children, but which does not appear in the vocabulary of the pursuer of the intuitive lifestyle, is "deserve." Intuitive people do not say, "She got what she deserved," and they would question the old Yorkshire proverb, "The sheep that hangs around the wolf's door deserves all it gets." What can such a proverb mean?

When people say deserve, they are usually imputing some moral quality to the action. Deserve usually implies a reward or punishment for doing good or doing bad. Hanging around a wolf's door is, for a sheep, bad behavior, as it will bring the sheep no good. For most of us raised in the western world, many of our actions are made to take on such a moral tone. Some actions are labeled moral and virtuous; others, immoral, sinful, or blameworthy. Laziness, lying, cheating, and stealing fall into the first category. Charity, study, and hard work fall into the second.

According to our western view, when one is charitable, one is rewarded—eventually at any rate, because that is what one deserves. Therefore, in this vein it follows that when one steals, one deserves punishment. We now offer you a different viewpoint.

In Chapter 4 we pointed out that floods or contagious diseases deal with all creatures impartially without regard to which ones are industrious or lazy. Indeed we say that such words have no part in the world of Nature. Now we are saying that these words have no part in the human world either, at least when that world is approached intuitively.

Just as nuclear fusion, osmosis, gravitation, and photosynthesis are not "actual" processes in Nature, but words we use to attempt to account for our observations of Nature, so also charity, theft, and diligence are not the actions themselves of people but the names we give to those actions. The intuitive person recognizes that living harmoniously both with Nature and with other people involves her coming into contact with their actions, and encouraging them to come into contact with hers, without intervening labels. How an act is labelled is essentially independent of how the participants in the act felt during and afterward. Is it an atrocity or an act of mercy to shoot injured horses, to remove life systems from a comatose loved one, to voluntarily terminate one's own pregnancy? Certainly the latter two issues have already polarized Americans. It is not what we call it, but how we feel about it that establishes an act as either an atrocity or an act of mercy, and it is that feeling that is too often forgotten in courtroom bargaining and bickering over pleas and procedure. In these issues of national significance, what we must be sensitive to is the part played in the various positions by given rules—rules phrased in terms of right and wrong, good and bad, should and ought, we versus they, believers in our particular set of rules versus non-believers and infidels. Actually, as you saw in the early chapters of this book, our current ethical and moral confusion has come, as much as anything, from humankind's love of rules, particularly the rules that divide us.

Neither people nor their actions ever deserve anything. Actions produce consequences, and it is only in that sense that the word "deserve" has any meaning to the individual living an intuitive lifestyle. When the Yorkshireman says, "The sheep that hangs around the wolf's door deserves all it gets," the intuitive person hears, "Hanging around the wolf's door has, in the past, had consequences for sheep that they have found most unpleasant!" People deserve what they get only in the sense that they themselves produce whatever happens to them. That is true even as far as the earthquake which almost kills you or the tornado which wipes out everything you cherish. If you do not believe this, ask yourself who made the various choices that led up to your being in the location of the earthquake or that tornado. The answer to your question, "What did I do to deserve this?" is, "Whatever it was that you did—that's what produced the 'this' that you're upset with."

To what extent do people produce whatever happens to them? In one sense, they are responsible for what happens to them since the actions leading up to the situation were theirs. However, many of us seem to resist this viewpoint. Indeed, in the United States to-day we all seem to be in a stampede away from responsibility and accountability. Everyone seems to be trying to make whatever goes wrong someone else's fault. Alcoholism, drug abuse, drug dealing, theft, vandalism, and violence against others is seen as the fault of a sick society, a broken family, having been abused as a child or, when all else fails, a disordered mind. And when the activity is "merely" white-collar theft, the defense against personal responsibility is that everyone is doing it. We have all been encouraged it seems (chiefly by those ultimate purveyors of rules, lawyers) not to accept responsibility for anything, certainly not for the unpleasant things that happen. Although, like the successful individual we spoke of in Chapter 8 we don't hesitate to take the credit (the opposite of blame) for the pleasant things that do occur.

It is as if people are saying, "I am not responsible for this injury, failure, loss, commission, or omission; somebody else is. It is as if people must blame someone, anyone, for a momentary failure in our desperate joint attempt to control our surroundings which has now caused injury. This is, in good measure, why we are a litigious society. But if, in order to achieve an orderly, calm, and predictable world, we continue to be willing to sacrifice the idea of the unfortunate accident that is no one's fault, we will soon find out, since we cannot have one without the other, that we have at the same time given up the possibility of the happy accident (such as the discoveries of the Salk polio vaccine, penicillin, radioactivity, and a hundred others).

There is, however, another view. The words blame, fault, and responsibility represent society's attempt to focus in one person all, or at least most, of the factors which brought about some undesirable event so that "justice" can be served. But neither your running away from responsibility nor your attempting through malpractice and negligence suits to fix responsibility on someone else are the answers. Fixing responsibility always requires arbitrarily selecting

a brief slice of time, ignoring what came before, and making a judg-
ment within that slice about who has the greatest share of the
blame for what happened. Time, however, and the myriad of
events in subtle and complex interplay which occur within it, cannot be cut into slices just to suit lawyers' views of how the world
ought to work. To do so, and to hold on to the notion that any
one person can be the entire focus of responsibility for anything,
goes against much that we have emphasized in this book. Whatever
happens: a break in a drought with needed rainfall, the discovery
of a vaccine, the development of a highly efficient clean energy
source, or a hurricane or an earthquake, are all the result of a
multitude of factors making up what we have called the "context."
The details and workings of this context, the contingencies, are indeed so complex and so subtle that we seem able to talk about only
some of them – and then usually in only roundabout and vague
ways. The rest of the context's workings we often ascribe to "God's
will" or the actions of some "higher power," in turn requiring of us
a humble willingness to grasp these strange ways in which "God
moves, his wonders to perform." We see this idea of an Act of God
in insurance claims following accidents where it has become impossible to fix sole responsibility or fault and, therefore, legal
liability (or moral blame) for the event.

Haven't you said, at least once in your life, "If I had to do it all
over again, I'd do it differently"? But would you? We doubt it. You
would not do things differently because you have always done
what you did based on

    (a) your past up until that moment in time,
and
    (b) the particular situation at hand.
If you could go back in time and be faced with the same situations
and choices, you'd do again exactly what you did the first time
through. And, if the exact same situation and choice faced you
now, you'd only deal with them differently because you've since
added to your fund of experiences.

What has all this got to do with whether or not we have responsibility for our actions? Just this: the very fact that now you'd do
some things very differently from the way you did them years ago

is a demonstration that it is the intervening experiences that are responsible for the change in your actions. It is as though you were a pawn in the hands of your interactions with surroundings. That, indeed, is the whole point of our book. You are, if not a mere pawn, then a piece, one of many on the chessboard we call the world.

However, you are a highly intelligent and thinking piece who, from time to time, is even able to describe how parts of that world work, and sometimes to alter those parts of the world to work for your own convenience and comfort. But most important, you are a being who, precisely because of your intelligence, thinks that you yourself and not your surrounding world, are responsible for where you find yourself, what you do and say about it and how you feel about what happens as a result. So long as you recognize that these alterations are no more than your accommodations to nature and not, as Sir Francis Bacon said, your "putting Nature to the rack," and so long as you recognize that what alterations you improvise are themselves influenced by your own past successes and failures with similar attempts, everything is fine. It is when you think that you, all by yourself, uninfluenced by past or present, can dictate to Nature, to the people in it, and to yourself, what you want, how things will work, what will happen, or how you'll feel, that stress, anger, and frustration begin. It is when you forget that your derived rules are from your experiences with Nature, and not to be dictated to Her as though they were rules you were giving Her, that difficulties emerge. That is when your passive solar house, a project of your own design, either gets unbearably hot by late morning even in mid-winter, or is much too cold at 5:00 A.M. the next morning.

It is when artists, writers, musicians, and design professionals think that they can be creative on demand or under the pressure of deadlines, when they think that they can, "command the muse to speak," that their labors result in ugly buildings and strange monuments. They then make weird canvasses and bizarre sculptures; unformed and cacophonous music and grotesque dances; plays, films, and TV dramatizations and sitcoms where violence and special effects substitute for substance and wit; and books whose sheer length and luridness of description of their multiple sexual encounters substitute for elegance of language, nuance of plot, subtlety of character, or irony of circumstance.

It is when we all collectively believe that we are totally responsible for what we can produce, predict, or control that real trouble starts. That is when women who have taken a drug to make them fertile give birth to six or more children; when underground water becomes polluted and rivers become sewers; species become extinct or undergo population explosions; forests are destroyed by acid rain; river deltas become infertile; mudslides bury villages; and the ozone layer is degraded.

It is just as misguided to impute total control, responsibility, and creativity to ourselves as it is to assign blame for our actions to a sick society or to having had divorced parents. No one of us, no matter how mature, independent, and "responsible" we become, ever escapes the subtle and pervasive influences of our surroundings, past or present. This is not to say that you have no control at all, or that you cannot optimize your chances for happy outcomes. You can, and that is the topic of the next chapter.

Summary

Acting intuitively means living every minute of your life recognizing that you are not the master of your fate; that you share with nature responsibility, credit, and even blame for what happens to you. There are countless unfathomed and unnamed contingencies having their say. And they have much to say regarding what you want, how you choose, where you find yourself, what and when you say, act, think, and dream the things that you do. You can influence these contingencies in both the social and in the inanimate world, but only inasmuch as you accommodate yourself to them. If you fight them, or attempt to dictate to them, you'll lose.

You are a part, a locus of activity, in a huge eternal cosmos most of whose workings are neither intrinsically hostile nor benign to us. They are only, for the most part, far beyond our puny minds to grasp.

Part 3

Your life thus far has likely been a product of your efforts at applying rules given to you by others, of your expectations, your intentions, your sense of justice, and your analyses of what was happening around you. You frequently expected the worst, and that is what happened.

In these final important chapters, you will learn that the key to obtaining positive results is simply to expect them. If you behave as if an outcome will be positive, you will sense Nature's guidance and influence the actions of others to effect the outcome you desire.

Your intuitive actions are the product of the totality of the world's contingencies. At the end of this final section, you will recognize that your major step in being comfortable with these contingencies is to release control, to let go of analyses and of attempts to control the future, and to relinquish guarantees of certainty. You will also see that you must not try to dictate to Nature how the scales of justice swing. If you allow life to happen rather than forcing it and planning it, you can create a beautiful, meaningful, stress-free environment in which you will thrive.

CHAPTER TWELVE

Affirmations: Facilitating Intuitive Action

"Our intention is to affirm this life, not to bring order out of a chaos
nor to suggest improvements in creation, but simply to wake up
to the very life we're living, which is so excellent once one gets one's mind
and one's desires out of the way and lets it act of its own accord."

John Cage

"Some things have to be believed to be seen."

Ralph Hodgson

"It does not matter what has been made of us; what matters
is what we ourselves make of what has been made of us."

Jan Kott

In the previous two chapters we have, we hope, convinced you that your own words are the chief obstacle to your dealing intuitively with your surroundings. This viewpoint has been in harmony with our emphasis throughout this book on the Taoist approach of wu-wei – of not-doing, and not-thinking – as your key to serenity, happiness, meaning, and fulfillment.

Wu-wei is undoubtedly difficult for many Westerners, reared as they have been in an assertive, striving, acquisitive, analytical, rational and, ultimately, frustrating, intimidating, and stressful approach to living. If we were to suggest "how-to" recipes and techniques, though, we would be violating the whole idea of an intuitive lifestyle, and falling back on rules and methods. This reluctance of ours has perhaps left some readers confused about where to begin. For these people, we offer the following in their transition to the accepting, passive, bending, releasing, yielding, peaceful, and gratifying way of an intuitive lifestyle.

When you feel you must think about how to deal with an unpleasant, stressful, or disappointing situation that you find yourself in, make a list of the expectations you originally had for the situation. For example, here is a set of expectations that a mid-level manager recently listed for a situation he saw as frustrating:

1. I expected top management to listen to my suggestions.
2. I expected to be kept informed.
3. I expected change to occur in the organization.
4. I expected incompetence to be punished.
5. I expected the leadership to have a clear program.

We have noted that expectations are futile and stress-producing. Indeed, having had such expectations as these above was almost surely the cause of that manager's unhappiness at his job. However, if those expectations are changed slightly, they can become "verbal facilitators" to help deal intuitively and productively with the situation. Such verbal facilitators we call affirmations. Below we have listed each of the manager's expectations, re-worded as affirmations:

1. Top management is listening to my suggestions.
2. I am being kept informed.
3. Change is occurring in this organization.
4. Incompetence is being punished.
5. Leadership does have a clear program.

What is the effect of making such statements of affirmation — of making an "inventory of an as-if present"? The effect is that it prompts you to act as though there were indeed no obstacles to your actions, no negative consequences, no disapprovals, no possibilities for "failure." And when you do act as if there were

no such obstacles, sure enough, at least some will turn out to be fig-
ments of your fears and doubts, and they will disappear, leaving
you once again to deal freely — that is intuitively — with your world.

You may feel that affirmations, inventories of an as-if present,
are mere self-deception, but they need not be. Return to our example. How can you say that things are not occurring in your organization which are the forerunners of your being kept informed, or
of the publicizing of the leadership's program without your knowing? Whether or not such is actually the case, your acting as if you
were happy (rather than frustrated or disappointed) with the situation will certainly prompt your superiors to tell you more than
they otherwise might, and lead them to listen to your suggestions
regarding program development or the organization's "dead wood."

Our example does have a happy ending. This manager, acting
with our advice, did reformulate his negatively-stated expectations
into positively-stated affirmations. He did start to act in harmony
with those affirmations and within a month or so of the change,
did receive a significant promotion which included reassignment
to the top ranks of the agency's hierarchy.

If you will make a list of your original expectations for what
has now become unpleasant, stressful, and disappointing for you,
and then reformulate each expectation into a positively stated affirmation, as demonstrated in our example, and then behave as if
those affirmations were true, we think that you'll be pleasantly surprised at the change in people's behavior towards you.

People generally feel the need to make affirmations when things
go wrong, just as they tend to pray, wish, hope, meditate, or just
plain worry at those times when life seems at its most frustrating
and depressing. They rarely feel the need to pray or to meditate
when they are sure of the situation — usually only when they are
unsure and confused. People pray, meditate, and make affirmations when the contingencies in the situation which confronts
them are unclear, and perhaps also seem dangerous. When situations are clear and the odds appear to be in your favor, you forge
ahead, you "go for it" unhesitatingly and with enthusiasm. People
don't then feel the need to pray or to search out obscure given
rules which they suspect may be hampering their effectiveness.

They don't ask advice from friends, or read how-to-do-it books in these circumstances. But when the coast is not clear, when contingencies are murky, they tread carefully.

This is true whether you are: looking down a steep snow-covered ski slope at Aspen or Stowe; looking up at a mountain's smooth rockface wondering whether you, your companion, and your climbing equipment are equal to the task; moving into a four-wheel drift at 110 miles per hour wondering whether you should have touched the brakes a little harder a few seconds ago; selling some excellent government bonds wondering if your assessment of how interest rates will move has been based on adequate information; or hesitating to talk to a very attractive stranger wondering if you'll be publicly embarrassed or humiliated. In every one of these cases, if you will reformulate your negative expectations into positive affirmations, things will turn out at least a little better than they would have if you had acted on the basis of your negative expectations.

But, you may say, being behind the wheel of a performance automobile is no time to make affirmations! And you would be absolutely right. Verbal affirmations are only a way-station, an interim measure you may feel the need to use in your transition to wu-wei, to not-doing and not-thinking. They are how you assert your share of control over your life. As long as you feel the need to talk to yourself to reassure yourself, about how to act in a particular situation, you have not yet reached wu-wei. Few people ever do!

Affirmations will over a period of practice become automatic, a habit, and eventually implicit, not stated at all. Your objective is to act "as if" everything will turn out for the best, almost as an "attitude" that all the contingencies are positive and rewarding. Those contingencies in the situation, even though you don't know it, will operate in response to your optimistic actions. What will happen? Sure enough, things will turn out OK. The negative possibilities in the situation will get much less of a chance to operate.

For example: "I am skiing this slope well; my climbing equipment is adequate to this rockface; my speed in this turn is OK for conditions; selling these bonds is advisable based on my best assessment of how interest rates will move; and this person is receptive to my talking to him/her." Affirmations, then, are statements that the situation you want already exists.

You are probably not surprised at this point of view. It is the position we have been taking throughout the entire book: that it is in the present where your actions are taking place, that all you need in order to act is here right now. It is only a small step from saying, "I will make it," to "I am making it," but what a difference in the feelings you have which accompany that statement.

Don't wish; don't set firm, clear goals; don't plan; don't even hope. Instead affirm!

If you are careful to set "hazy" goals, and if you then allow contingencies to freely play themselves out on all parties involved, what you want will happen. The route may be circuitous, though, and not by any direct route or mechanism you might have planned or even anticipated. It will just be by Nature's own way — in which you allow yourself to be a willing and vulnerable participant.

Summary

Living the intuitive lifestyle involves the continuous awareness of and sensitivity to the world's contingencies. Anything you might say can interfere with that sensitivity. Best to say nothing. But, as you are learning to be more intuitive, you may feel you must say something. Then, let it be an affirmation which states how that part of your world which is troubling you is also immediately ready to reward you, and that you are thankful that it is.

CHAPTER THIRTEEN

Releasing: The Rebirth of Intuitive Action

"We also draw together when we become aware that night must close in on all living things, that we are condemned to death at birth and that life is a bus ride to the place of execution. All of our struggling and vying is about seats on the bus, and the ride is over before we know it."

Eric Hoffer

The reader may wonder, now that we have reached the final chapter of our book, whether we have forgotten to include something that would seem to belong in any book dealing with intuitive action; that is, a discussion of where intuitive processes are located in the brain. While we hope that we have laid this issue to rest for most of our readers, there may be some who will be comfortable only with more explicit coverage. We will, therefore, make this brief digression.

You will have noticed that although we have talked at great length about intuitive action, the intuitive lifestyle, intuitive approaches to problem-solving, and indeed, subtitled our book *The Art of the Intuitive Lifestyle*, we have never used the word intuition as a noun. Our avoidance of the noun intuition has been deliberate. In teaching you how to act intuitively, we have taken the approach that it is the interplay between your actions and the world where your emphasis must be placed, and not in the search for some entity or thing or some mysterious process forever beyond your reach located in some mythical or psychical realm, or in one or the other of your cerebral hemispheres.

Let's face it, suppose that intuitive action were indeed controlled from within the right cerebral hemisphere, as some have suggested; and suppose further that we knew exactly where within that hemisphere that control was located. What then? We cannot now control any of the nervous activity within our brains. Not one neuron within the entire central nervous system can be "fired at will" by us. This is not true of neurons outside the central nervous system, which can be brought under our voluntary control particularly with the aid of biofeedback equipment. But not the workings of the central nervous system.

This means that, so long as you believe intuitive action to be controlled by the central nervous system, of which the cerebral hemispheres are an important part, you cannot change that control; you cannot learn how to be more intuitive. Regardless of how many so-called experts have said that you can "tap into the right hemisphere," it still remains for them to tell you just how to do that, and for them to be sure that is what you are actually doing when you are acting intuitively. The central nervous system (the undamaged central nervous system, including both sides of the brain connected to one another and not "split" as in the research studies of R. W. Sperry) is involved in no special way with intuitive activity. The intact central nervous system is there all the time, working away as a whole, regardless of the specific activity in which you're involved.

Actually, looking for "thoughts" or for evidence of "learning" physically within the brain is an example of what philosophers call category error, or the confusion of universes of discourse. This means that words like thinking, dreaming, (the) mind, imagery, and memory belong to one category or universe, while words like brain, cortical hemisphere, and neuron belong to quite another. It is perfectly permissible to talk within either category, using the terms that are appropriate to it. It is when we cross over from one category to another and we co-mingle words like memory with words like cortex, using them in the same sentence as though they belonged to the same category, that we get into trouble. Such a misuse of words, particularly when they are nouns, gets us quickly started on a search for things which simply are not there.

Our favorite expression of this view is that of Tristan Tzara, the Romanian-French poet and founder of the Dadaist school which inspired artists such as Chagall, Klee, Dali, and Miro, sculptor Giacometti, and musician Erik Satie. Tzara said, "La pensee se fait dans la bouche," ("Thinking happens in the mouth.").

The most famous of these confusions is the "Mind-Body" problem. Philosophers have grappled unsuccessfully with this for at least two thousand years. The problem is: "How can the mind, which has no substance and takes up no space, influence the body, which does?" (Thinking about certain things can, over a long enough time, give you an ulcer). And, the other way around, "How can the body influence the mind, as we see by so many examples that it can?"

This whole question is a pseudo-problem, born out of the confusion of two universes of discourse. Mind and body are nothing less than two fundamental ways of looking at everything that exists in nature. There is the "mind" way of looking at things, and there is the "body" way. Dreams and thoughts are part of the mind way; and nerves, the brain, and the adrenal glands are part of the body way. There is no connection, no link at all, between them. They are just like the English System of weights and measures (inches, pounds, gallons) and the Metric System (meters, grams, and liters): each system can operate entirely without the other.

It is not the brain that thinks, nor even the mind; it is we who think—we as entire beings. As Woody Allen says in the film, *Manhattan*, "the brain is the most overrated organ."

Some writers on the subject of intuition have suggested that it is made up of four component processes: preparation, incubation, illumination, and verification. This is nonsense. Just as intuition is not an entity or a thing as its representation in our language as a noun might suggest, neither are incubation, etc., entities or things. Suggesting that there is such a "thing" as "preparation" as a component process of an entity called intuition is only the overactive wishful thinking of writers who believe that special psychic or neuro-mechanical processes in the brain must underly the actions

133

we call intuitive. These writers are the kind of people whom the political philosopher John Stuart Mill was thinking of when he said:

> "The tendency has always been strong to believe that whatever received a name must be an entity or being, having an independent existence of its own. And if no real entity answering to the name could be found, men did not for that reason suppose that none existed, but imagined that it was something peculiarly abstruse and mysterious."

Intuitive action is action influenced by the totality of the world's contingencies, free of your own explicit and intended attempts to control — nothing more, and nothing less. And now to its rebirth!

The "Human Condition," that seemingly never-ending tension between what is and what you think ought to be, between the good and evil which seems to emerge from everything you do, can be met squarely. But it can be met squarely only by letting go of your notions of should and ought. Your stress, discontent, boredom, your sense of the meaninglessness and the purposelessness of life, your sense of isolation and despair, of loneliness and emptiness, is not inevitable.

This human condition becomes "The Human Comedy" (the phrase is Balzac's) only because humans insist on struggling against the world instead of yielding to it. "Thy will be done," say the pious as they personify all that is ineffable in nature. It is human nature to be free, to be creative, intuitive, even mystical, and to be intimate with and a part of Nature. "Man," as Jean-Paul Sartre said, "is condemned to be free." It is when you try to limit the risks of being free, when you invoke recipes, criteria, plans, policies, procedures, and rules — particularly given rules, and formulas for future action that you violate your essential humanity and cause yourself stress. You regain that freedom and you escape stress when you let go of such rules.

Hence this book has had one over-riding theme: Living a life free of stress, frustration, and despair — a life filled with meaning, personal fulfillment, and contentment – involves no special technique, formula, or method. It does not involve your starting to do certain things that have thus far been missing from your life and which, if you started doing them, would add the missing ingredients of happiness and success. At most it involves a "way."

Your stress is due to there being too much in your life – to your trying to deal with too much, and not too little. The key, then, is to continuously release and let go of those many things that you have been trying desperately and unsuccessfully to hold on to and to control. You have been trying to control the uncontrollable; to be responsible for things for which only Nature, Herself, can be responsible.

What we will do in this last chapter is to summarize the many areas in which you may be trying to hold on.

Let go of many of your given rules. Given rules, what we've also called the universal statements of should and ought, are the guides for living which you picked up as you were growing up, and they are usually implicit, i.e., unconscious. They tell how you ought to act, how things ought to be, what should happen, etc. Search them out, however you can, examine them, and either confirm, modify, or reject them.

Let go of your attempts to control the actions of others. The best way to influence others is first to acknowledge their wants as legitimate; that is to validate them. As a young acquaintance once argued many years ago during a particularly heated teen-parent duel, "If you want to reward me, give me something I want – not something you want me to have or something you think I ought to want!" When you attempt to control the actions of others in other ways, such as by threats, arguments, bribery, appeals to family ties or to old emotional debts, you will have an uphill battle and you will put yourself under considerable stress. And you will fail.

The two parties in any relationship become truly free when each lets go of attempts to control the other's actions; when each says to the other, "Do what you think is best for you." Then the person who hears that statement is set free to act in his or her best interest, and the speaker of those words is set free of any feelings of responsibility he or she may feel if things turn out badly for the other.

You must also let go of a dependence on others which goes beyond the principle noted above. In that way you will also be free of the worry whether or not the person you depend upon will come to your rescue if things don't turn out well. Being free of stress means being free of dependence.

Also you must let go of your need to have others feel about something the way you do. If you like chamber music, or baseball, or hiking, or roller derbies, it is not necessary that those around you do, too. Nor does their contempt and ridicule for your hobbies and pastimes disqualify them from playing any other part in your life.

We must not only let others be free, we must also remove obstacles to our own freedom. This is nowhere made clearer than in mid-life career changes where you may still want to hold on to some of the benefits and "perks" of your earlier lifestyle: the socially prominent friends, the elegant wardrobe, the expensive car, the fine home, the diplomas and certificates—some of which may mean nothing in your new career. But if you choose to be free of stress, if you approach life intuitively, the vestiges of your earlier life, whatever they are, may have to be released.

Let go of analysis. Analysis is our word to describe the western approach to understanding the world we live in. It includes logical approaches, data analysis (especially these days through the use of computers), and reason and rational argument. Trying to understand everything that happens, everything that people (including yourself) do and say, is a futile, and therefore stressful, effort. Let go of that need to understand why.

Let go of your need to control the future. This is another futile and therefore highly stressful enterprise, yet people try to do it all the time. They plan, contrive, propose, commit, promise, and predict. And then they watch in frustration and impotence as Nature disposes of their cherished hopes and dreams. Be content to share control only of the present. Take care of now as best you can. Then, when tomorrow arrives, at least you'll have no residual unfinished business left over to hamper your efforts at dealing with whatever tomorrow has brought.

Let go of guarantees of certainty. Allied with the need to control the future is the need for a guarantee that things will be a particular way. This need in some people is so strong that they latch onto a particular viewpoint or theory as "the answer" to whatever it is that they have been searching for. Nothing, absolutely nothing, that has any bearing on how you live your life, is certain. If you are to live a life free of stress, you must let go of the need for guarantees of that certainty.

Let go of intention. Intending to do something, as oppposed to just doing it, is planning, and planning is only a more formal, i.e., rule-regulated, method of controlling the future. Let go of intending to do something; just do it.

Let go of "decision-making." As we have pointed out, decision-making is, unlike an inventory of the present which occurs before you make your choice, frequently only a masquerade. It attempts to legitimize intuitive choice by pasting a veneer of data, logic, computer models, or whatever on top of an action that has already been chosen. Go ahead and act intuitively; without feeling the obligation to justify it after the fact with contrived facts and figures.

Let go of "what you will do if..." This is yet one more device to escape the present and to try to live in the future, to decide how you'll act then. But you can't possibly specify all the contingencies that will be operating at that time and, even if you could, you still couldn't say for sure what you would do. The intuitive person waits to see what happens and, continuously inventorying that present, then acts in such a way as seems appropriate.

Let go of firmly defined goals. Goals can be problematic whether or not they are attained. If they are too specific, or if they are held on to too firmly, they can hamper your intuitive actions. If you must have goals, keep them vague and be ready to alter them. Focus on how you want to feel when you attain them, not on the outcome itself. Perhaps other things can make you feel the same way.

Let go of labeling and of giving meaning to the actions of others. This is akin to analyzing and understanding why others do what they do. To the extent that you label people, or give your own meaning to what they have done, you restrict your ability to deal intuitively with both the people and their actions. Let go of your labels. Deal with people's actions as they present themselves to you.

Related to this is the holding on to the conditions under which you will love someone, or under which someone will presumably love you ("You would if you loved me;" "You wouldn't have if you loved me."). The reasons why people do things, or do not do things, may be only distantly related to whether or not they love you. Be careful of making such an analysis of another's actions. Like most of your other analyses, it is almost certainly superficial at best.

Let go of trying. Trying is related to intending and also to decision-making. When you try to do something, say, ride a horse, you're doing something different from just riding that horse. It is that extra effort implied by the word trying that is stressful. And it is that word trying that prevents your actions from being intuitive. Intuitive people don't try, they just do or, as we have been saying, they just not-do! They do not try to ride a horse, they mount up!

Let go of hurt. Remember that some people enjoy holding on to hurt. They resist every opportunity to let it go, to reconcile with the person who supposedly inflicted the hurt. They sometimes even seem to try to make the hurt last longer than it might. One wonders if they are not thereby explicitly avoiding doing what would effect a reconciliation. Let hurt go! Holding on to it will hamper your dealing intuitively at least with similar situations by making the hurtful event more significant than it needs to be.

Let go of blame, recrimination, revenge, and vindication. If you are going to live a stress-free, fulfilling, serene, and intuitive life, these motives, these given rules for action, must be let go. You cannot right the balance. You cannot decide what part your idea of "justice" should play in the affairs of humanity. In the eyes of some, you are perhaps the transgressor.

Let go of the need to take full credit. Just as you cannot assign blame to others, you cannot take the credit yourself for what happens. This is because the responsibility for what happens lies in good measure outside you, in the vast context with all its subtle contingencies in constant interplay. Since you are not solely responsible for what you did, how can you take the full credit for it? See yourself as a facilitator of Nature's way.

Let go of "mistakes" as well as "successes." Success and failure can only be determined after the fact; that is, in the future. But, at

the moment you are acting, despite what the pattern of consequences appears to have been in the past, you can't know for sure
what the consequences will be this time. And it is those consequences which will, later on, be the basis for someone's deciding
whether or not your action was a "mistake" or a "success."

Let go of formal expectations. Remember the section of Chapter 5 where we asked, "Who would have predicted...?" We suggested that a considerable source of your stress is the continuing
violation of your specific expectations: your expectation that the
United States will always be "Number One," your expectation that
people will act on your advice when they asked for it, your expectation that if you work hard, things will go well for you, etc. The
way to escape this source of stress is not to make more accurate
predictions or to have more "realistic" expectations. It is to have no
defined expectations at all. Let the future go!

There is a second kind of expectation that must also be released: expectations of you by others. As long as others' expectations are accepted and agreed to by you, perhaps also backed up by
an offer of something you want in return for the thing expected of
you, OK. If not, let them go.

A third kind of expectation to release is the expectation that
things will always turn out badly for you. You do this by following
our recommendations in Chapter 12. Look at the positive possibilities in situations, and act as if there are no negative contingencies.

Let go of what you are holding in your mind. This is certainly
the most difficult to do of all the things we've suggested: the clutter
and "noise," the details and trivia that make up much of what you
think about each waking moment. Let it all go! This harks back to
our discussion of *mizu no kokoro* and *tsuki no kokoro*, those states of
mind cultivated by the oriental martial arts experts, which emphasize clarity, sensitivity, awareness, calmness, openness, and respon-
siveness. Remember that in the West, saying that a person has lost
his or her mind is saying that the person is crazy; but in other
cultures, a person with no mind is considered wise, sensitive, kind,
and fulfilled.

Develop routines to lighten your load. Don't try to remember
trivia. Write things down in order to "forget" them. "Do it now," is

good advice because it keeps your mind clear and enables you to deal less encumbered and therefore more intimately and more effectively with your world. The key word is not "relax;" it is "release." Let go, and become invulnerable.

This world of ours is indeed hard to deal with, but it is the world as it is; there is no other. And, in great measure, it is a world which all of us and our forebears have created, albeit unwittingly. Whether or not it was ever meant or supposed to be anything else, whether it should be any different from the way it is, is irrelevant. This is it.

Things are not beyond hope, however; far from it! Life can still be beautiful, free of stress, meaningful, happy, and filled with accomplishments if we do not try to understand it, to explain it, analyze and rationalize it. Life doesn't make sense. It doesn't have to for you to find fulfillment. Besides, what your mind cannot grasp, your body, your entire being, has already figured out. Perhaps, as was suggested by the quote at the beginning of the book, God is indeed a comedian and we are indeed afraid to laugh. After all, who is the joke on?

Suggested Reading

Bach, Richard D. (1977). *Illusions: The Adventures of a Reluctant Messiah*. New York: Dell.

Browne, Harry. (1973). *How I Found Freedom in an Unfree World*. New York: Avon.

Burden, Virginia. (1957). *The Process of Intuition*. New York: Greenwich Book Publishers.

Capra, Fritjof. (1982). *The Turning Point*. New York: Simon and Schuster.

Carse, J. P. (1986). *Finite and Infinite Games*. New York: MacMillan.

Cornuelle, Richard. (1975). *De-Managing America*. New York: Random House.

Fetzler, W., and Field, Eleanor S. (1985). *The Good Girl Syndrome*. Berkley Brooks: New York.

Hoff, Benjamin. (1982). *The Tao of Pooh*. New York: Dutton.

Holmes, E. and Kinnear, W. H. (1959). *A New Design for Living*. Englewood Cliffs, New Jersey: Prentice-Hall.

Miller, C. and Swift, K. (1976). *Words and Women*. Garden City: Doubleday.

Payne, David. (1984). *Confessions of a Taoist on Wall Street*. Boston: Houghton Mifflin.

Shawn, Wallace and Gregory, Andre. (1981). *My Dinner with Andre*. New York: Grove Press.

Siegel, B. S. (1986). *Love, Medicine, and Miracles*. New York: Harper and Row.

Siu, R. G. H. (1980). *Transcending the Power Game: The Way to Executive Serenity*. New York: Wiley.

Vaughan, Frances E. (1979). *Awakening Intuition*. Garden City: Doubleday.

About the Authors

The authors of *Warm Logic* have been working together for four years.

Louis Wynne was raised in the industrial north of England during and after World War II. He came to the United States as a teenager, later served in the U.S. Air Force, and then trained as a psychologist at Ohio State. While working first in human and animal research laboratories, then eventually in psychiatric hospitals and mental health agencies, he became convinced that traditional scientific methods of understanding action, thinking, and feeling were misguided. He saw that helping people in emotional distress did not seem to be a matter of technique. Dr. Wynne came to feel that our culture is at a turning point at which the rational, analytical science in which he had been trained was now doing more harm than good, both to our environment and our fellow creatures, as well as ourselves.

Dr. Wynne realized that a new, more contextually sensitive approach was needed—one which gave prominence, rather than the back seat, to intuitive processes. He now maintains a clinical and consulting practice in Albuquerque, New Mexico, in which the ideas in *Warm Logic* are applied.

Carolyn Klintworth was raised in the mountains of east Tennessee, attended high school in the atomic city of Oak Ridge, and graduated from George Peabody College of Vanderbilt University. Her formal training was in Fine Arts and Biology. She subsequently trained in the field of Developmental Disabilities, in which she has now worked for many years, establishing innovative training programs.

143

Carolyn has spent much of her life in the out-of-doors, observing and feeling the balance and harmony that exist in the forests and fields. She translated these ways of life into concepts woven throughout this book.

Her mountain traditions, melded with the cold logic of science, culminated in the concept of *Warm Logic*. Drawn to the spiritually charged energy of the Southwest, she eventually made her home in Santa Fe, where she began consciously defining and practicing the art of the intuitive lifestyle.

Carolyn currently is Administrator of a large residential facility for persons with developmental disabilities in New Mexico.

This Book

Cover design by Robert Pawlack
Designs, San Francisco. Typogra-
phy by Camille, El Paso, Texas.
Text set in Goudy Old Style,
headings set in Romic Light.
Printing by Malloy Lithograph,
Ann Arbor, Michigan.
A SKIDMORE-ROTH PUBLICATION

THE NEW AGE AFFIRMATION CALENDAR

This inspiring, day-by-day calendar features one uplifting affirmation for each day of the year. Special affirmations are geared to holidays. reflecting the positive spirit of each event. Calendar pages include: • an affirmation at the top • the day, week, and year in striking, large type • a small inset calendar that shows the month at a glance • holiday notations • plenty of space for taking notes or jotting down reminders. *The New Age Affirmation Calendar* is an ideal gift and the perfect means for overcoming doubts and worries, and for enhancing self-esteem, goals, and serenity every day of the year.

$8.95, Daily calendar, ISBN 0-944132-06-5
Calendar, 365pp, 4½ x 5¼

Skidmore-Roth Publishing

"I am enjoying every aspect of my life"

NEW AGE
AFFIRMATION
CALENDAR

BY ELIZABETH MOORE

NUMEROLOGY
The Language of Life
Ruth Drayer

Numerology
The Language of Life

Ruth Drayer

Simple, easy-to-understand guidelines explain all aspects of numerology and give readers actual examples of the use of this science of numbers.

This guide offers a fascinating, informative look at the scientific basis of numerology as developed by L. Dow Balliett, the originator of numerology. The book is arranged by number, and gathers in one place information about birth paths, personalities, heart desires, and planes of expression, providing readers with a feeling for the characteristic or "personality" of each symbol.

Written for the beginning numerologist, this book is easy to read, yet gives an in-depth understanding, including a complete sample chart for an individual. Contents include: "A Little of the History of the Science of Name and Number," "Terms and Definitions," "The Master Numbers," "The Inclusion Table," "Planes of Expression," "Free Will," "Name Changes," "Birthdays," "Personal Cycles," and more.

Ruth Drayer lives in Las Cruces, NM.

May, $11.95, Trade paper, ISBN 0-944132-12-X
Occult/New Age, 200pp, 6 x 9

Skidmore-Roth Publishing

CLIP AND SEND

____ Numerology: The Language of Life $11.95

____ New Age Affirmation Calendar $8.95

Name _____

Address _____

City_____ State_____ Zip_____

Phone: (   ) _____

☐ Visa   ☐ Mastercard   ☐ American Express
☐ Check/Money Order Attached

Card # _____

Expiration Date _____

_____
SIGNATURE

Please add $3.00 each postage and handling. Please add local sales tax.

Skidmore-Roth Publishing
207 Cincinnatti Ave. El Paso, Texas 79902 • 915-544-3150